Baseball is more than a game to me, it's a religion.

—Bill Klem

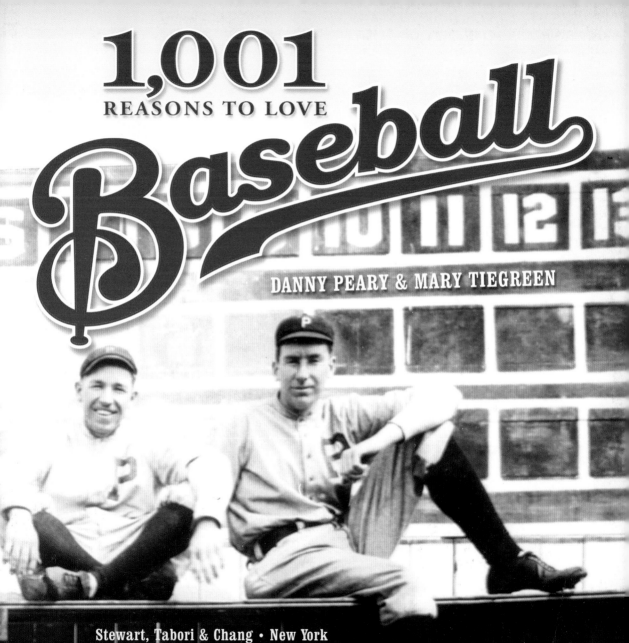

1,001
REASONS TO LOVE
Baseball

DANNY PEARY & MARY TIEGREEN

Stewart, Tabori & Chang · New York

Published in 2004 by
Stewart, Tabori & Chang
A Company of La Martinière Groupe
115 West 18th Street
New York, NY 10011

Export sales to all countries except Canada, France, and French-speaking Switzerland:
Thames and Hudson Ltd.
181A High Holborn
London WC1V 7QX
England

Canadian Distribution:
Canadian Manda Group
One Atlantic Avenue, Suite 105
Toronto, Ontario M6K 3E7
Canada

Library of Congress Cataloging-in-Publication Data
Peary, Danny, 1949-
1,001 reasons to love baseball / Danny Peary.
p.cm.
ISBN 1-58479-354-6
1. Baseball-Miscellanea. 2. Baseball-Pictorial works.
I. Title: One thousand one reasons to love baseball.
II. Title: One thousand and one reasons to love baseball.
III. Title.
GV867.P43 2004
796.357-dc22

Design concept by Mary Tiegreen
Cover and interior designed by
David Green/Brightgreen Design
Photo Editor: Anne Kerman

1,001 Reasons to Love Baseball is a book
in the 1,001 REASONS TO LOVE™ Series.

1,001 REASONS TO LOVE™ is a trademark
of Mary Tiegreen and Hubert Pedroli.

ISBN: 1-58479-354-6

Printed in China

10 9 8 7 6 5 4 3 2 1
First Printing

CONTENTS

Introduction **8**

THE GREATS

INTRODUCTION

I fell in love with baseball before first sight, long before I could talk in full sentences. By the time I was five I was a baseball-card-carrying member of Young Baseball Fanatics of America, studying the faces of my first heroes, memorizing a ridiculous number of statistics, and wanting someone—anyone—to throw a baseball in my direction. The pleasures of baseball were so clear to me that I couldn't understand why every other kid didn't live and breathe the game, too. I assumed it was the birthright of the American child to bond with baseball, but apparently I was mistaken. Years later, when I met adults who had somehow grown up in a baseball-free environment, or had been turned off to the sport at an early age, I felt they had been deprived of untold joys. Everyone should experience playing ball with a motley group of neighborhood kids; smacking and catching a ball; opening a bubblegum-scented pack of trading cards; following a favorite team and a special player's entire career; watching a million games on TV; and finally, going to a game at a major league park.

Baseball to me is really about cumulative memories of playing the game and being a fan. People who meet baseball for the first time as adults are at a disadvantage; they have no existing history to which they can add the new experience. That's why it is extremely hard to convert adults to the game. But I have made it my mission to keep trying by subjecting countless people—including my foreign-born relatives—to repeated exposure. I say, "Forget the opera, and come to a night game with me!" This book will, I hope, remind diehard, longtime baseball fans why they love this exciting, aesthetically beautiful, multi-faceted game so much, because its pages include an accumulation of baseball memories we all share. Equally important, I believe that it will help them explain to their naïve acquaintances, through pictures and words—1,001 of the reasons I have used on converts of my own (including Mary Tiegreen)—why it makes sense to have such passion for the game. Maybe they will come to realize that few things in life are as satisfying as America's pastime.

—Danny Peary

the card that changed my life

1 Baseball is America's pastime

[Baseball] will take our people out-of-doors, fill them with oxygen, give them a larger physical stoicism. Tend to relieve us from being a nervous, dyspeptic set. Repair these losses, and be a blessing to us.

—Walt Whitman

Lou Gehrig and Babe Ruth

Baseball was, is, and always will be to me the best game in the world.

—Babe Ruth

* * * * *

2

All teams, good and bad,
are tied for first place
on Opening Day

3

Skipping school or calling
in sick to go to the park
on Opening Day

4

U.S. presidents
attending Opening Day
in Washington, D.C.

5

Walter Johnson pitching
14 season openers for the
Washington Senators
—7 of them shutouts

* * * * *

14

6

Even though it's still
winter where you live,
spring training
is underway

7

Pitchers and catchers
reporting to camp

8

Taking vacation days to
see spring training games

9

When injured players
return for a new season

10

Getting a first glimpse
of a young phenomenon

11

The Grapefruit League
and the Cactus League:
the exhibition competitions
during spring training in
Florida and Arizona

12

Making preseason
predictions

Now all you fellers line up
alphabetically by height.

—Casey Stengel

13 You've got tickets and the weatherman says,
"It's going to be a great day for a ball game."

14
Fireworks Night

15
The time-honored tradition of booing the umpire

16
Checking the scoreboard to see how all
the other games are progressing

17
A colorful grounds crew sweeping
the infield between innings to the beat
of loud stadium music

18 Playing ball till the sun goes down

19 Seeing kids play ball as you drive through a town you've never been to before

20
When the winning run
is 90' from home plate

21
When the infield plays "in"
to cut off a run at the plate

22
When a left-handed batter
is challenged by a great
left-handed pitcher

23
When the batter,
in a split second,
determines the spin and speed
of the pitch and swings
— or not

The left side of the brain controls the right half of your body, and the right side controls the left half. Therefore, left-handers are the only people in their right minds

— Bill Lee

24
Kids swinging as hard as they can
in case they hit the ball

25
The challenge of getting a hit,
the hardest thing to do in any sport

26
Somehow making contact on an "unhittable" fastball

27
When the coach yells to the overeager young batter
"Wait for your pitch!"

28
The idea expressed by many great hitters
that in every at-bat, you will get at least one pitch
that is hittable

* * * * *

29
Hank Aaron

* * * * *

Overcame racial prejudice to break
Babe Ruth's "unbreakable" record
of 714 career home runs,
finishing with 755

Holds career records
with 2,297 RBIs and
6,856 total bases

Played without flair or fire,
but with greatness

Was the last player
from the Negro Leagues
to play in the major leagues

Clinched the 1957 pennant
for the Braves with an 11th-inning
homer against St. Louis

* * * * *

30
Barry Bonds

✳ ✳ ✳ ✳ ✳

Ranks with Willie Mays and Joe DiMaggio
as one of the 3 best all-around players
in baseball history

Slammed an eye-popping 73 home runs
in 2001 to break McGwire's
1998 seasonal record

Holds the record for MVP awards

Is the son of outstanding player
Bobby Bonds and godson of Willie Mays

Is the only player in history to hit
500 homers and steal 500 bases

Improved as he got older

✳ ✳ ✳ ✳ ✳

31 Roger Maris's beautiful, quick, left-handed swing
—ideal for Yankee Stadium

36
The symmetry when the infielders are in their natural positions
and outfielders play "straight away"

37
60' 6" equals perfection — the distance from the mound to home plate

38
90' equals perfection — the distance between the bases

39

The whiteness of the baselines and bases at the beginning of the game

40

When they used to play Sunday doubleheaders

41

Photos of old ballparks

★

TEAM NAMES OF LONG AGO

★ ★ ★

42
Boston Beaneaters

43
Boston Pilgrims

44
Brooklyn Bridegrooms

45
Brooklyn Tip-Tops

46
Chicago Orphans

47
Chicago Whalers

48
Cleveland Spiders

49
Elizabeth Resolutes

50
Houston Colt-45s

51
Louisville Eclipse

52
New York Highlanders

53
Pittsburgh Rebels

54
Seattle Pilots

55
St. Louis Perfectos

56
Troy Haymakers

ONLY HALF THE TRICK

Bruce took the 2 strikes, and he leaned in and waited for the curve, and it come, and it was maybe an inch or 2 out, and Bowron called it a ball, Cleveland beefing hard, and the crowd as well, and I remember Dutch crying above the sound, "Good eye, Pearson," Bruce leaning on his bat and waiting for Cleveland to calm, and then stepping back in, his jaw working and saying, "Rob McKenna is only a country boy like me, or else a country boy from the city," Rob looking down at Coker on first, then looking in, and kicking and pitching. Bruce counting on the curve, set for it, swinging, and when he hit it you knew it was hit and never looked for it, Coker tearing for second full speed and then slowing and jogging on around and waiting at the plate for Bruce, and shaking his hand. Longabucco sat down, and I took my swipes, looking for the 2 strikes first, and then the curve, and swinging on the curve, but fanning. The damn trouble is that knowing what is coming is only half the trick. You have still got to hit it. We took it, 3-2.

Mark Harris, *Bang the Drum Slowly*

TEAMS AND TEAMMATES

61
New York Giants, 1926
with future Hall of Fame infielders:
first baseman George Kelly, second baseman
Frankie Frisch, shortstop Travis Jackson,
and third baseman Freddie Lindstrom.

62
Oakland A's, 1970s
A's owner Charles O. Finley paid
his players to grow mustaches during
the 1970s, which resulted in their
nickname, the Mustache Gang.

63
Brooklyn Dodgers, 1947-53
The Brooklyn Dodgers had 4
National League Rookies of the Year:
Jackie Robinson, Don Newcombe,
Joe Black, and Junior Gilliam.

64
Newark Eagles, 1930s
The Negro Leagues' Newark Eagles
had a "Million Dollar Infield," comprised
of mammoth slugger Mule Suttles, Dick
Seay, and future Hall of Famers
Ray Dandridge and Willie Wells.

65
St. Louis Cardinals, 1930s
The wild and woolly Gas House Gang
of the Cardinals included Pepper Martin,
Frankie Frisch, Leo Durocher, Ducky
Medwick, and pitchers Dizzy
and Daffy Dean.

✶　✶　✶　✶　✶

Travis Jackson and Frankie Frisch

66

Yankee pinstripes

67

The St. Louis Cardinals' logo

68

The Arizona Diamondbacks'
purple cap with the D in
the shape of a snake

69

Lou Gehrig's Yankee
number 4 was the first
athlete's number ever retired

70

Hank Aaron, who wore
number 44, hit 44 home runs
in 4 different seasons, and his
record-breaking 715th career
home run was given up by Al
Downing, who also wore 44

71

Bill Voiselle,
a pitcher from Ninety-Six,
South Carolina, wore
number 96

72

Eddie Stanky and
Ron Hunt, who wore
baggy uniforms so they
would be hit with
pitches more often

73

Jackie Robinson's
number 42, which has
been retired throughout
the major leagues

74

Oscar Gamble's huge Afro,
which barely fit under his
baseball cap in the 1970s

75
Walter Johnson

* * * * *

Arguably the fastest pitcher
in major league history

Throwing only a fastball, led the
American League in strikeouts 12 times

Won 417 games pitching for the
infamously bad Washington Senators

Was the winning pitcher as a reliever
in the final game of the 1924 World Series,
giving the Senators their only title

Holds the record with 110 shutouts

Was called the Big Train

* * * * *

COSMIC BALL

**Being on the mound puts me
in a relaxed state of super-
consciousness. The feeling is laid
back, but still intense. Everything
is slowed down, yet you are able to
perceive things at an incredibly fast rate.
Line drives shot up the middle may look hard
to the observer in the stands, but they never
seemed dangerous to me. They floated to
the mound in slow motion. When your arm, mind, and
body are in sync, you are able to work at peak
performance level, while your brain remains relaxed.
It's Zen-like when you're going good. You are the ball
and the ball is you. It can do you no harm.**

—Bill Lee

Some days you tame the tiger, and some days the tiger has you for lunch.

—Tug McGraw

76 Tim Hudson

SENSATIONAL PITCHERS OF THE 21st CENTURY

* * *

77 Mike Mussina	**83** Bartolo Colon	**89** John Smoltz
78 Roy Halladay	**84** Greg Maddux	**90** Andy Pettitte
79 Mariano Rivera	**85** Randy Johnson	**91** Russ Ortiz
80 Barry Zito	**86** Curt Schilling	**92** Kerry Wood
81 Pedro Martinez	**87** Kevin Brown	**93** Mark Prior
82 Mark Mulder	**88** Eric Gagne	**94** Jason Schmidt

95
Randy Johnson

* * * * *

At 6'10", is the tallest
pitcher in major league history

Is the most intimidating
left-handed pitcher ever

Makes a hobby of setting
strikeout records

Started and relieved
to help Arizona win the title
in a 7-game World Series against
the Yankees in 2001

* * * * *

Talent makes winners, not intangibles. Can nice guys win? Sure, nice guys can win— if they're nice guys with a lot of talent. Nice guys with a little talent finish fourth, and nice guys with no talent finish last.

—Sandy Koufax

Johnny Podres

PITCHING FEATS

* * * * *

96
Johnny Podres, 1955
The Brooklyn Dodgers won their only world title,
finally beating the New York Yankees in the
World Series, when Podres pitched
a shutout in Game 7.

97
Carl Hubbell, 1934
In the All-Star Game, Hubbell struck out 5 other future
Hall of Famers in succession: Babe Ruth, Lou Gehrig,
Jimmie Foxx, Al Simmons, and Joe Cronin.

98
Lew Burdette, 1957
Burdette pitched 3 complete game victories
over the powerful New York Yankees to lead the
Milwaukee Braves to victory in the World Series
over the defending champions.

99
Ralph Terry, 1962
Yankees pitcher Terry got the final out
in the World Series with Game 7 on the line,
2 years after giving up the game-losing homer
in the 7th game of the 1960 World Series.

* * * * *

The basis of intimidation, as I practiced it, was a mystery. I wanted the hitter to know nothing about me .... That was why I never apologized for hitting anybody.

—Bob Gibson

100
Bob Gibson, 1968
The Cardinals' Gibson threw 13 shutouts and had an ERA of just 1.12, the 3rd lowest of the 20th Century and lowest after the dead-ball era.

101
Rube Marquard, 1911
Marquard won 19 straight decisions as a starter, still the record.

102
Jesse Orosco, 1979-2003
Orosco, who debuted in 1979 and was still pitching in 2003, has made more appearances than any pitcher in history.

103
Pedro Martinez, 1999
At the All-Star Game at Fenway Park, Boston's Martinez struck out the first 4 National League batters of the game and 5 of the 6 batters he faced.

104
Early Wynn, 1963
Dead-armed Wynn stubbornly struggled for several months to achieve his 300th and final victory and a guaranteed induction into the Hall of Fame.

★ ★ ★ ★ ★

105
Don Newcombe, 1956
Newcombe, major leagues' first outstanding black pitcher,
had a 27-7 record and became the first pitcher to win
the Cy Young Award and MVP in the same season.

106
Harvey Haddix, 1959
Pittsburgh's Haddix threw a record 12 perfect innings
against the Braves, but then yielded a hit, a walk, and a run
and ultimately lost, 1-0, in 13 innings.

107
J. R. Richard, 1978
Houston's Richard, who could throw 100 mph,
became the first National Leaguer to strike out 300 batters
—and he did it again the next year.

108
Old Hoss Radbourn, 1884
Radbourn won 60 games in that year, and 311 games
in his 11-year career, almost 30 a season.

109
Sam Jones, 1955
The Cubs' Jones walked the bases loaded to begin
the 9th inning against the Pirates, but then struck out
the next 3 batters to preserve his no-hitter.

★ ★ ★ ★ ★

Don Newcombe

110
Grover Cleveland Alexander, 1915-1917
Became the only pitcher to lead the league in wins,
ERA and strikeouts 3 years consecutively.

111
Grover Cleveland Alexander, 1916
Alexander also became the last pitcher to win
as many as 33 games in one season.

112
Matt Kilroy, 1886
Kilroy struck out 513 batters, a record
that will never be broken in the modern era.

113
Tim Keefe, 1880
Keefe is the only starting pitcher in baseball history
to give up less than a run a game for a season
—his 0.86 ERA will never be broken
in the modern era.

★ ★ ★ ★ ★

Grover Cleveland Alexander

It ain't braggin'
if you can do it.

—Dizzy Dean

114
Dizzy Dean, 1934
Dean was the last pitcher in the National League to win 30 games.

115
Whitey Ford
Ford won more games than any Yankee pitcher in history
and threw 32 consecutive scoreless innings in the World Series.

116
Warren Spahn
Spahn won 20 games in 13 different seasons for the Braves
and set a record for lefthanders by winning 363 games.

117
Johnny Vander Meer, 1938
Cincinnati's Vander Meer threw 2 consecutive no-hitters,
a record that will never be broken.

118
Karl Spooner, 1954
At the end of the season, Spooner began a very short-lived career
by pitching 2 complete games for the Brooklyn Dodgers, shutting out
both opponents while giving up only 7 hits and striking out 27 batters.

★ ★ ★ ★ ★

119
Tom Seaver, 1970
Seaver struck out a record 10 batters in a row to end a game.

120
Orel Hershiser, 1988
Hershiser, of the Dodgers, pitched 59 consecutive innings
without yielding a run.

121
Steve Carlton, 1972
Carlton won 27 of the last-place Phillies' 59 victories.

122
Tom Cheney, 1962
Cheney, of the Senators, struck out a major league record 21 batters
in a 16-inning victory over Baltimore.

123
ElRoy Face, 1959
Face won 18 of 19 decisions and had a record
.947 win-loss percentage—as a reliever!

✫ ✫ ✫ ✫ ✫

Tom Seaver

124

Cy Young,
who won more games (511)
than any pitcher in history

PITCHES

* * *

125
A four-seamer fastball—
high and the hardest thrown

126
A two-seamer fastball that sinks

127
A split-fingered fastball—like a change-up,
but with the bottom falling out

128
A wicked slider that breaks parallel to the ground

129
An effective curveball that breaks downward,
with the 12-to-6 curve being the best

130
Stu Miller's changeup, which he threw
with the same motion as his fastball
but about 30 mph slower

* * *

FASTBALL

CURVE

CHANGE-UP

131 **Christy Mathewson**

Won 373 games, tying for the most in National League history

Won 37 in a season, the National League record

Threw 3 shutouts in the 1905 World Series

His "fadeaway" pitch was the predecessor to the screwball

Went to college and dressed and acted like a gentleman in an era of ruffians

Christy Mathewson pitching, 1913 World Series, Philadelphia, Pennsylvania

MATHEWSON, N. Y. NAT'L

61

132 The legendary New York Yankees of the 1920s, led by Babe Ruth and Lou Gehrig

133 The Yankees' "Murderers Row" lineup

134 New York won 0 world titles before acquiring Babe Ruth; they've won 26 since

135 The 1927 Yankees—perhaps baseball's greatest team

There are no two cities
in America where the
people want to beat each
other's brains out more
than in San Francisco
and Los Angeles.

—Red Sox Hall of Famer
 Joe Cronin

GREAT RIVALRIES

* * * * *

* * * * *

CONFRONTATIONS

* * * * *

142
In an exhibition game in 1967, softball wizard
Eddie Feigner whiffed 6 consecutive batters,
including future Hall of Famers Willie Mays,
Willie McCovey, Brooks Robinson, Roberto
Clemente, and Harmon Killebrew

143
Ted Williams crushed Rip Sewell's "eephus pitch"
for a long home run in the 1947 All-Star Game

144
The intimidating Don Drysdale
versus the fearsome Willie McCovey

145
Reggie Jackson versus Bob Welch

* * * * *

**Good pitching will always stop
good hitting and vice-versa.**

—Casey Stengel

146
A pitcher's duel

147
No-hitters

148
The rare perfect game

149
A relief pitcher
getting out of a jam

150
A pitcher winning
his 20th game
of the season

151
That the spitball
was once legal

152
The inventor
of the curveball was
a 19th century catcher,
Candy Cummings

153
The inventor of
the split-fingered
fastball, pitching coach
Roger Craig

154
The "Big Mitt" that
Baltimore Orioles catchers
used to help them catch
Hoyt Wilhelm's knuckleball

155
A great pitching coach,
Johnny Sain

156
The knuckler, which is
held by the fingertips,
not the knuckles

✷　✷　✷

The way to catch a knuckleball
is to wait till it stops rolling
and then to pick it up.

—Bob Uecker

Eric Gagne

157 **Lights-out closers**

WHO WAS BETTER?
(1950s)

158
Catchers Yogi Berra
or Roy Campanella

159
Centerfielders Mickey Mantle,
Willie Mays, or Duke Snider

160
Shortstops Phil Rizzuto
or Pee Wee Reese

161
The Yankees pitchers
or the Dodgers pitchers

162
The Yankees, Dodgers,
or Giants, team for team

Those debates continue...

163
Ty Cobb

The best "pure hitter" ever

Retired in 1928 with 90 American League
and major league records

Still holds the mark for highest
career average and ranks in the top 5
in games, runs, hits, total bases, doubles,
triples, RBIs, and stolen bases

Was legendary for his meanness,
yet established a medical center and
an educational fund

* * * * *

Baseball was one-hundred percent of my life.
— Ty Cobb

164
The passion for baseball in Japan

✴ ✴ ✴

165
The popularity of baseball
in South Korea

166
Baseball played by kids in Taiwan

167
Baseball played in Australia

168
The popularity of baseball in Mexico,
the Dominican Republic,
and Puerto Rico

169
People who never cared about baseball
turning into fans when their home team
suddenly becomes a contender

Hideki Matsui
and Ichiro Suzuki

Baseball is a lot like life. The line drives are caught, the squibbles go for base hits. It's an unfair game.

—Hot Rod Kanehl

Babe Ruth and Ernie Shore

170

Baseball Trivia

$\star$ $\star$ $\star$ $\star$ $\star$

A What Boston Red Sox owner sold Babe Ruth to the Yankees?

B Who was the only starting pitcher to have an ERA under 2.00 during the 1950s?

C On what 2 teams were Preacher Roe and Billy Cox teammates?

D Who was the pitcher when Roger Maris hit his record 61st home run in 1961?

E What was Johnny Mize's nickname?

F Which Dodger did not win the National League Rookie of the Year Award —Jackie Robinson, Roy Campanella, Don Newcombe, or Junior Gilliam?

G On May 2, 1917, what did pitchers Fred Toney of the Reds and Hippo Vaughn of the Cubs do?

H Who caught Hank Aaron's 715th home run?

I Who played third base for the Cubs with shortstop Joe Tinker, second baseman Johnny Evers, and first baseman Frank Chance?

J Since Ted Williams batted .406 in 1941, who has recorded the highest single-season batting average and what was it?

See page 208 for answers

BASEBALL LINGO

★　★　★

171 PAY-OFF PITCH—the pitch delivered when there is a full count

172 Small Ball—scratching out runs in what promises to be a low-scoring game

173 Wheelhouse—area where the hitter can unload on a pitch

174 Can of Corn—a fly ball that is easy to catch

175 Texas Leaguer—a bloop hit that lands just past the infield

176 *Frozen Rope*—a low line drive that doesn't change height after initial contact

177 Cup of Coffee—a brief stay in the majors

178 Hot Corner—third base, because so many hard hit balls go that way

179 *Pull the String*—a pitcher throws the ball with his fastball windup and delivery but grips the ball farther back in his hand so, when released, it will go much slower than the batter expects

180 NOSEBLEED SEATS—the highest level in the stadium seating area

181 BOB UECKER SEATS—nosebleed seats in the very last row, where Bob Uecker was given a free seat in a television ad

182 *Gopher Balls*—home-run pitches, so called by Lefty Gomez because they "go fer" homers

183 DUCKS ON THE POND—base runners

184 FULL COUNT—three balls and two strikes

185 *Firemen*—relief pitchers, because they douse the flames of an impending rally

186 STOPPERS—starting pitchers whose victories repeatedly end their teams' losing streaks

✦　★　✦

187 ***A 55-Footer***—a pitch that lands in front of home plate, which is 60' 6" from the mound

188 **THE 40–40 CLUB**—the few players who have hit 40 homers and stolen 40 bases in the same season

189 **The Mendoza Line**—the .215 average, poor-hitting Mario Mendoza hit in his career and what every hitter wants to hit far above

190 ***"He rang 'im up"***—used by broadcasters when the umpire calls a third strike

191 **Hit for the Cycle**—to get a single, double, triple, and homer in the same game

192 **Baltimore Chop**—a batted ball that hits on or near home plate and bounces high in the air, giving the batter enough time to reach first base safely

193 **The Neighborhood Play**—pivot men at second base will get a force out call by most umpires if their foot is close to the base—in the neighborhood—before they throw to first base

★ ★ ★

194 THE BASH BROTHERS—Oakland A's slugging teammates Mark McGwire and Jose Canseco, from 1986 to 1992

195 The Nasty Boys—intimidating relievers Randy Myers, Rob Dibble, and Norm Charlton of the Cincinnati Reds in the early 1990s

196 Billy Ball—a fun, aggressive style to scratch out runs that was initiated by manager Billy Martin of the weak-hitting Oakland A's in the early 1980s

197 Whitey Ball—a winning, exciting style of baseball played on Astro-turf and built around speed and defense that was the creation of manager Whitey Herzog with the Kansas City Royals and St. Louis Cardinals

198 TOOLS OF IGNORANCE—the gear worn by catchers, who play their position despite being victimized by foul tips, wildly bouncing balls, bats, and collisions

199 TOOLS OF INTELLIGENCE—what former catcher Tim McCarver calls the same gear, worn by the players who must understand the game better than anyone else on the team

THE AMERICAN NATIONAL GAME OF BASE B

GRAND MATCH FOR THE CHAMPIONSHIP AT THE ELYSIAN FIELDS, HOBOKEN, N.J.

* * * * *

200

Elysian Fields in Hoboken,
New Jersey, was the site of the first
baseball game under a set of rules

201

Baseball was played
by soldiers during the Civil War

202

The first professional team was the
rowdy Cincinnati Red Legs in 1869

203

Before 1881, pitchers threw
underhanded from 45 feet away

* * * * *

204
Tossing the ball back and forth
on the front lawn after dinner

205
Every game includes something
you've never seen before

206
When your dentist turns out
to have been a former
major leaguer

207
Pennant races that go down
to the final day

208
When your team is at the top
of the standings

209
Baseball in the sun
or under the lights

210
Foul poles are in fair territory

211
Upsetting the best team
in the league

212
A nail-biting, extra-inning game

213
The annual Little League and
College World Series

* * * * *

214
The anticipation while waiting
in the on-deck circle

215
On-deck batters swinging
several bats

216
Studying the pitcher
from the on-deck circle

217
Great switch hitters

218
Great designated hitters

219
A slugger comes up
with the bases loaded

* * * * *

We sometimes seem to save our greatest devotion for those heroes who don't quite make it, or who lose gallantly, or who have flaws. Mickey Mantle more than fit the image.

—Robert W. Creamer

Since baseball time is measured only in outs, all you have to do is succeed utterly; keep hitting, keep the rally alive, and you have defeated time. You remain forever young.

– Roger Angell

220
Alex Rodriguez

SENSATIONAL HITTERS OF THE 21st CENTURY

* * *

221
Barry Bonds

227
Vladimir Guerrero

233
Gary Sheffield

222
Jason Giambi

228
Nomar Garciaparra

234
Garret Anderson

223
Luis Pujols

229
Derek Jeter

235
Jim Thome

224
Sammy Sosa

230
Mike Piazza

236
Frank Thomas

225
Todd Helton

231
Miguel Tejada

237
Ichiro Suzuki

226
Carlos Delgado

232
Manny Ramirez

238
Rafael Palmiero

All I want out of life is that when I walk down the street folks will say, "There goes the greatest hitter that ever lived."

—Ted Williams

TED WILLIAMS
outfield BOSTON RED SOX

Ted Williams

239
Ted Williams

* * * * *

Was the last player to bat over .400 when he hit .406 in 1941

Refused to sit out the season ending doubleheader in 1941
at the risk of going below .400, and went 6 of 8

Hit a 3-run, 9th-inning homer to give the American League
a 7-5 victory in the 1941 All-Star Game

Served in both WWII and the Korean War, preventing him
from getting 600 home runs or 3,000 hits

Hit .388 at the age of 40

Homered in his last at-bat and made no curtain call

Was surrounded by adoring current players on the field
prior to the 1999 All-Star Game

240
A perfect bunt

★　　★　　★

241
A sizzling liner

242
A fly ball that stays up forever

243
A leadoff walk,
which usually leads to a run

244
Smacking a ball past
a drawn-in infielder

245
Productive outs that score runners
or move them up a base

246
How cunning batters figure out
what the pitcher will throw next

247
The wonderful clicking sound
as the ball is hit by the
"sweet part" of the bat

248
The challenge of trying
to hit a round ball squarely
with a curved bat

249
Taking batting practice

250
Hitting off a pitching machine

251
When a batter swings
as hard as he can in anticipation
of a fastball but gets a
change-up instead

Pedro Martinez

THE DIVIDING LINE

Though I couldn't play baseball worth a damn, I loved baseball statistics. I spent hours poring over the league batting averages in the Sunday papers. Baseball was something I could worship bookishly in private along with all the other trivia one found in newspapers and almanacs. To this day, I can name all the presidents and most of the state capitals. But in my childhood I did not know that the cumulative score of every baseball game ever played averaged out to five runs for the winning team and three runs for the losing team. Hence, the significance of the 3.00 earned run average as a dividing line between good and bad pitching, and by somewhat more arcane calculations, of .300 as the dividing line between good and bad hitting.

—Andrew Sarris

HITTING FEATS

* * * * *

252

George Brett, 1976, 1980, 1990

Brett became the only player to win batting titles in each of 3 decades.

253

Don Mattingly, 1987

Mattingly became the only player to hit 6 grand slams in a season.

254

George Brett, 1980

Brett batted .390, the highest average since Ted Williams batted .406 in 1941.

255

George Brett, 1980

The Kansas Royals reached the World Series for the first time when Brett hit a 3-run, 7th-inning home run against Goose Gossage to erase a 2-1 deficit for a 3-game sweep of the Yankees in the ALCS.

256

Don Mattingly, 1986

Mattingly set New York Yankee records with 238 hits and 53 doubles.

257

Dale Long (1956), Don Mattingly (1987), and Ken Griffey, Jr. (1993)

Each homered in a record 8 consecutive games.

* * * * *

* * * * *

258
Sammy Sosa
Became the first player to have 3 seasons
with more than 60 homers to his credit.

259
Sammy Sosa
Also holds the National League record
with 6 straight 40-homer seasons.

260
Alex Rodriguez
Of the American League also has 6 straight
40-homer seasons.

261
Babe Ruth
Set the major league record by blasting
over 40 homers in 7 straight years.

262
Harmon Killebrew
Hit over 40 homers in 8 seasons,
leading the league 6 times.

* * * * *

Monte Irvin

263
Monte Irvin
Batted over .400 3 times in the Negro National League.

264
Wee Willie Keeler
Keeler had over 200 hits in 8 consecutive seasons,
and once batted .424.

265
Rusty Staub
Was the first player to have 500 hits for 4 different teams:
the Expos, the Mets, the Rangers, and the Tigers.

266
Rod Carew
Won 7 American League batting titles and was the 6th player
to hit over .300 for 15 consecutive years.

267
Honus Wagner
Led the National League in hitting 6 times from 1903 to 1909
and finished 2nd the other year.

268
Rickey Henderson
Hit a record 81 leadoff homers.

* * * * *

269

Jimmie Foxx, 1932

Hit the most homers in the majors in the 1930s, had 58 homers
in 1932, only 2 shy of Babe Ruth's record, and 534 in his career,
which was second to Ruth until 1966.

270

Jimmie Foxx, 1932, 1933, 1938

Won 3 MVP awards with the Athletics and Red Sox.

271

Jimmie Foxx (1932–1940) and Rafael Palmeiro (1995–present)

The only players to have 35 homers and 100 RBIs in 9 straight seasons.

272

Shawn Green, 2002

In a game against the Brewers, Los Angeles outfielder Green
went 6-for-6 with 6 runs scored and 7 RBIs, a record-tying 4 home runs
and 19 total bases, a new major league record.

273

Joe Adcock, 1954

At Ebbets Field against the Dodgers, Milwaukee's Adcock
swung the bat 5 times and had 4 homers and a double.

* * * * *

Jimmie Foxx

Ernie Banks

274
Ernie Banks
Banks won 2 National League MVP awards although
the Cubs tied for 5th place out of 8 teams.

275
Joe Carter, 1993
Carter homered off the Phillies' Mitch Williams
in the 9th inning of Game 6 of the World Series
to give the Toronto Blue Jays a world title.

276
Chris Chambliss, 1976
Chambliss's homer over the right-field fence
in the bottom of the 9th inning in the final game of
the ALCS against Kansas City's Mark Littell's gave the
New York Yankees the American League pennant.

277
Jim Thome
Nice guy Thome of the Indians slugged 2 homers
in a game to fulfill a promise to a hospitalized boy
he had befriended.

278
Sadaharu Oh
Slugged 868 homers in Japanese baseball, a world record.

* * * * *

Ralph Kiner

279
Ralph Kiner, 1946–1952
Kiner set a record by leading or tying for the lead in homers
for 7 consecutive seasons.

280
Gabby Hartnett, 1938
Hartnett won the pennant for the Cubs by breaking a 5-5 tie
with a 9th-inning roundtripper off Pirates' ace reliever Mace Brown.
On an 0-2 count, just before the umpires were about to call
the game on an account of darkness, he hit what became
known as the "homer in the gloamin'."

281
Carl Yastrzemski, 1967
The Red Sox clinched the American League pennant on the last day
of the season, as Yastrzemski went 4-for-4 to finish as a Triple Crown
winner with 44 homers, 121 RBIs, and .326 average.

282
Dick Sisler, 1950
Sisler's 10th-inning home run against the Dodgers won the National League
pennant for the Phillies on the last day of the season.

283
Mike Schmidt, 1976
On April 17, 1976, the Phillies erased a 13-2 deficit to the Cubs at Wrigley Field
and won 18-16 on Schmidt's record-tying 4th home run of the game.

✶ ✶ ✶ ✶ ✶

284
Bill Mazeroski, 1960
Pittsburgh's Mazeroski hit the first home run in history
to end a World Series, when his 10th-inning blast off Yankees
pitcher Ralph Terry won Game 7 of the Series.

285
Wade Boggs, 1983–1989
Boston's Boggs had 7 consecutive 200-hit seasons.

286
Pinky Higgins, 1938
Higgins became the first player to get 12 straight hits,
walking twice in his 14 plate appearances.

287
Walt Dropo, 1952
Detroit's Dropo got 12 straight hits in 12 plate appearances.

288
Tommy Agee, 1969
In Game 3 of the World Series, Mets center fielder Agee
homered and saved 5 runs with 2 amazing catches.

289
Hugh Duffy, 1894
Duffy batted .438, the all-time record.

✳ ✳ ✳ ✳ ✳

Bill Mazeroski

290

Carlton Fisk waved his arms to "push" his long fly ball fair in the bottom of the 12th inning and give the Red Sox a victory over Cincinnati in Game 6 of the 1975 World Series—the ball hit the net attached to the foul pole for a game winner.

✳ ✳ ✳ ✳ ✳

291
Stan Musial, 1948
Musial led the National League in batting average, slugging average, total bases, runs, RBIs, hits, doubles, and triples, and came within one home run of winning the Triple Crown.

292
Tony Oliva, 1964–65
Minnesota's Oliva became the first player to win batting titles his first 2 years in the majors.

293
Larry Walker, 1997–1999
Colorado's Walker hit .366 in 1997, .363 in 1998, and .379 in 1999 to become the first hitter since Al Simmons, from 1929-1931, to bat over .360 for 3 straight years.

294
Rogers Hornsby, 1924
Hornsby batted .424, the highest average of 20th Century.

295
Brady Anderson, 1996
Anderson smashed 50 home runs as Baltimore's leadoff hitter.

✳ ✳ ✳ ✳ ✳

296
Mark McGwire

☆ ☆ ☆ ☆ ☆

Hit 70 home runs in 1998 to obliterate
Roger Maris's major league record of 61

Befriended the family of Roger Maris

Started out as a pitcher

Hit a rookie-record 49 homers in 1987
for the Oakland A's

Regularly hit 500-foot homers in St. Louis

Turned down most endorsements
after setting the record

Retired without fanfare because injuries
limited his performance

☆ ☆ ☆ ☆ ☆

297

Seeing your favorite player in person for the first time

★ ★ ★ ★ ★

298 Wearing your favorite team's cap

299 A date at the ballpark

300 It didn't rain as expected and the game is on

301 Keeping score at the ballpark

302 An usher lets you move to a better seat

303 Giveaway promotions

304 Batboys and ballgirls

305 The ballpark organ music

306 When the entire family goes to the ballpark

307 Igniting a rally by yelling "Charge!"

308 A 9th–inning, come-from-behind rally

309 A star player breaking out of a slump with a big hit

310 Great players who make baseball look easier than it really is

311 Fans applauding an opposing player

312

Hank Greenberg

Remains the preeminent Jewish batter in baseball history

Endured much anti-Semitism and became the most prominent
Jewish symbol and hero of the 1930s

Hit 58 homers, falling 2 short of Babe Ruth's major league record,
and had 183 RBIs, one shy of Lou Gehrig's American League record

Was the second player to enlist in the service in WW II

After 4 years in the serviee, he returned to homer in his first game
and on the last day of the season slammed a 9th-inning grand slam
to give Detroit a 6-3 victory and the American League pennant

Albert Pujols

313
A perfectly executed hit-and-run

314
A pinch-hit home run

315
A red-hot batter

316
Breaking up a no-hitter

317
A great comeback

318
A rally

319
The way batters
in the first inning
use their feet to rub
out the back line
of the batter's box

320
When the worst player
gets the biggest hit

321
A great hitting coach,
like Charlie Lau

322 Stan Musial

Called "Stan the Man"

Started out as a pitcher and became the best hitter in the National League in the 1940s and early 1950s

Had 3,630 hits—of which 1,815 were hit at home, and 1,815 were hit on the road

Hit a 12th-inning homer to win the 1955 All-Star Game

Won 3 MVP awards, including one in 1948 when he led the league in 8 offensive categories

Always a genial guy who loved to shake hands and play the harmonica

DO THE MATH

Ralph [Kiner] had a natural home-run swing. All he needed was somebody to teach him the value of hard work and self-discipline. Early in the morning, on off-days, every chance we got, we worked on hitting.

"Let me ask you something," I said to him. "In a 150-game season, let's say you go to bat four times a game. That's 600 times at bat. Let's say you get two decent swings each time at bat. That's 1,200 swings. If you stand here at home plate and you make the pitcher throw strikes, don't you think that with 1,200 swings you'll hit 35 balls out of the park?"

"Sure," he said.

"Well," I said, "that's all there is to it. You know you're going to get 1,200 swings. Now the secret is to make the pitcher throw strikes. If you learn the strike zone, you're automatically going to have 35 home runs a season. It's as simple as that."

He learned the strike zone and instead of hitting 35 home runs, he hit over 50 twice and led the league seven straight years. Except for Babe Ruth, no one has ever hit as many home runs per time at bat as Ralph Kiner.

—Hank Greenberg in *The Glory of Their Times*

323 "Home Run" Baker

BURNS, BATTER, BALTIMORE.

MEMORABLE NICKNAMES

✭ ★ ✭

324
Amos "the Darling" Booth

325
Oyster Burns

326
Johnny "Trolley Line"
Butler

327
Oil Can Boyd

328
Pickles Dillhoefer

329
Charles "Old Hoss"
Radbourn

330
Tony "Poosh 'Em Up"
Lazzeri

331
Pop Corkhill

332
Baby Doll Jacobson

333
Bris Robotham
"the Human Eyeball" Lord

334
Peanuts Lowrey

335
"Rawmeat Bill" Rodgers

336
William Van Winkle
"Chicken" Wolf

337
Nick "Tomato Face" Cullop

338
Roger "the Duke of Tralee"
Bresnahan

339
Peek-A-Boo Veach

340
Jim "Catfish" Hunter

341
Willie "Puddin' Head" Jones

342
John "the Count"
Montefusco

343
Ewell "the Whip"
Blackwell

344
John "Pretzles" Pezzullo

345
Frankie Frisch,
"the Fordham Flash"

346
Rabbit Maranville

347
Bow Wow Arft

348
Al Hrabosky was
"the Mad Hungarian".

349

Yankee pitcher Ed Lopat was called
"the Junkman"
because of his ugly assortment of pitches.

350

Mike Hargrove took so long
before he stepped into the batter's box
before each pitch that he was nicknamed
"the Human Rain Delay".

351

Red-haired Rusty Staub was dubbed
"le Grand Orange"
when he played for the Montreal Expos.

352

Brothers Paul and Lloyd Waner were
"BIG POISON" AND "LITTLE POISON".

353

Yankees pitcher Vic Raschi was
"THE SPRINGFIELD RIFLE";
the Brooklyn Dodgers strong-armed
right fielder Carl Furillo was
"THE READING RIFLE".

354

George Selkirk was called
"Twinkletoes"
because he ran on
the front of his feet.

355

Brooks Robinson scooped up so many
difficult grounders that he was called
"the Vacuum Cleaner".

356

Charles "Lady" Baldwin
got his nickname because
he didn't smoke, drink, or swear.

357

5'9" Astros outfielder Jimmy Wynn
had so much power that he was called
"the Toy Cannon".

358

19th century outfielder Jack
"Death to Flying Things"
Chapman got his nickname because
he caught the ball barehanded.

★　　　　　　　　　★

How can I intimidate batters if I look like a goddamn golf pro?
—Al Hrabosky

1968 ROOKIE STARS

METS

JERRY KOOSMAN • P   NOLAN RYAN • P

stan musial

MICKEY MANTLE
Micky Mantle

Yankees

PIRATES

BOB CLEMENTE
OUTFIELD

CAL RI...
3rd

BALTIMORE
FUTURE STA...

126

Collecting baseball cards

360
Opening a new pack
of baseball cards

361
Getting your favorite player
in a pack of baseball cards

362
Having two of a valuable card;
one to keep and one to trade

363
Getting the card of the rookie
who is tearing up the league

364
Valuable rookie cards

365
Cards from the
19th century

366
Finding a box of old cards
in your grandparents' attic

367
The umpire cards in
Bowman's 1955 set

368
Putting together
a full set of cards

369
Flipping cards

370
A mint set of cards

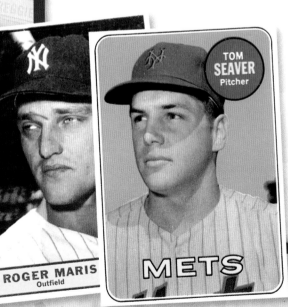

★ ★ ★ ★ ★

371
Card shows and shops

372
The 1952 Topps card of
Mickey Mantle, the most
prized card issued after
World War II

★ ★ ★ ★ ★

373
The mystique of
Honus Wagner's rare 1909
tobacco card, worth more
than a million dollars,
and the highest-priced
item of memorabilia
in baseball

374
1955 Bowman baseball
cards, in which the players
are shown inside color
televisions

375
Finding the card you've
been searching for

★ ★ ★ ★ ★

129

* * * * *

376

The All-American Girls Baseball League, which existed for 12 years beginning in 1943

377

Women in the All-American Girls Baseball League slid into bases although they were required to wear skirts

378

The all-female Colorado Silver Bullets played baseball against men's teams from 1994 to 1997

379

Tim McCarver learned to hit low pitches at the age of 3 when his older sister rolled balls to him

* * * * *

380
Boston pitcher Bill Lee learned the screwball from his aunt Annabelle Lee, who pitched in the All-American Girls Baseball League

381
Helen Callahan St. Aubin, of the All American Girls Baseball League, and her son Casey Candaele, who reached the major leagues in the late 1980s, are the only mother-son duo to play professional baseball

* * * * *

Tops IN GIRLS SPORTS

ACTION! GLAMOR!   TRAVEL! THRILLS!

★ ★ ALL-AMERICAN GIRLS BASEBALL LEAGUE ★ ★

PLAYING WITH THE GIRLS

I might as well just take a deep breath and come right out and put the matter bluntly: the team I started with was the Bloomer Girls.

Yeah, you heard right, the Bloomer Girls....

In those days there were several Bloomer Girls teams that barnstormed around the county.... The girls were advertised on posters around Ness City for weeks before they arrived, you know, and they finally came to town and played us and we beat them.

Well, after the game the fellow who managed them asked me if I'd like to join and finish the tour with them ... and he offered me $20 if I'd play the infield with them those last three weeks.

"Are you kidding?" I said.

"Listen," he said, "you know as well as I do that all those Bloomer Girls aren't really girls. That third baseman's real name is Bill Compton not Dolly Madison. And that pitcher, Lady Waddell, sure isn't Rube's sister. If anything, he's his brother!"

"Well, I figured as much," I said. "But those guys are wearing wigs. If you think I'm going to put a wig on, you're crazy."

"No need to," he says. "With your baby face you won't need one anyway."

Fact is, there were four boys on the team: me, Lady Waddell, Dolly Madison, and one other, the catcher. The other five were girls. I think everybody except maybe some of the farmer boys must have known some of us weren't actually girls, but the crowds turned out and had a lot of fun anyway. In case you're interested, by the way, the first team Rogers Hornsby ever played on was a Bloomer Girls team, too. So I'm not in such bad company.

—Smoky Joe Wood in *The Glory of Their Times*

382

Ilsa Borders was the first woman to win a college baseball game
at Southern California College in 1994, and the first woman to pitch
in a men's professional baseball game as a member of the St. Paul Saints
in the independent Northern League in 1997

383

In an exhibition, female pitcher Jackie Mitchell struck out Babe Ruth
and Lou Gehrig on 6 pitches

384

Lizzie Murphy, Babe Didrickson, and other women who played
in exhibition games against male ballplayers

BASEBALL MOVIES

★ ★ ★

385

Bang the Drum Slowly (1973)

Poignant tale of the friendship between smart, protective star pitcher
Michael Moriarty and his simple-minded catcher Robert De Niro,
who the entire team rallies around when he is struck by a fatal illness.

386
Alibi Ike (1935)
Baseball fanatic Joe E. Brown is Ring Lardner's hero,
a cocky Chicago Cubs hurler who won't face up to his mistakes.

387
Angels in the Outfield (1951)
Manager Paul Douglas needs assistance from heaven to make the Pittsburgh Pirates
—with cameos by the real players—pennant contenders.

388
The Bad News Bears (1976)
Crotchety, beer-drinking Walter Matthau becomes manager
of a hapless Little League team and Tatum O'Neal becomes its star pitcher.

389
The Bingo Long Traveling All-Stars and Motor Kings (1976)
Pre-WWII Americana about a barnstorming team comprised of talented
renegades from the Negro Leagues.

390
Bull Durham (1988)
Ex-minor leaguer Ron Shelton wrote and directed this tribute to the minors,
with Kevin Costner, Tim Robbins, Susan Sarandon (as a groupie), and Robert Wuhl.

391

Damn Yankees (1958)

Washington Senators players sing "You Gotta Have Heart," but their new star player sold his soul to the devil in order to help his favorite team beat those damn Yankees.

392

Eight Men Out (1988)

Period piece by writer-director John Sayles (who also plays Ring Lardner) about how and why 8 Chicago White Sox players threw the 1919 World Series.

393

Fear Strikes Out (1957)

Jimmy Piersall complained that Anthony Perkins "threw like a girl," but otherwise he gave a riveting performance as the young outfielder who had to overcome mental illness before becoming one of the majors' most memorable players.

394

It Happens Every Spring (1949)

Ray Milland takes his place next to spitballers and greaseballers as a professor who becomes a pitching star after he invents a substance that makes balls avoid bats.

395

The Life and Times of Hank Greenberg (2000)

Documentary about how the Hall of Famer withstood anti-Semitism to become the greatest Jewish hitter in history.

396

Major League (1989)

Director-writer David Ward gave up waiting for the Cleveland Indians to win a championship, so he made this comedy with funny baseball scenes, oddball characters, and Bob Uecker spoofing broadcasters.

397

The Natural (1984)

Robert Redford portrays a baseball player who tries to make it as a pitcher and then a hitter while dealing with moral dilemmas—with an upbeat ending, unlike the original novel.

398

The Pride of the Yankees (1942)

This biography has good baseball scenes, including an appearance by Babe Ruth, and a fine romance between Gary Cooper's Lou Gehrig and Theresa Wright's Eleanor Gehrig.

★　　★　　★

399
The Sandlot (1993)
A shy, young boy tries to fit in with
the close-knit kids on a sandlot team.
A sweet film about a childhood
rite of passage.

400
Take Me Out to the Ball Game (1949)
Gene Kelly and Frank Sinatra are ballplayers
in this turn-of-the-century musical, playing for
owner Esther Williams, and singing
a show-stopping "O'Brien to
Ryan to Goldberg."

You spend a good piece
of your life gripping a
baseball, and it turns
out it was the other way
around all the time.

—Jim Bouton

401
A new, unmarked ball

402
Getting a star to sign your ball

403
Perfecting grips for different pitches

404
The wonderful sensations of hitting,
throwing, and catching a ball

405
The coach dumping out a bag
of used balls before practice

406
Used major league baseballs
—each one with a history

* * * * *

407
Teaching your younger brother or sister
how to hit and throw

408
Hearing praise from someone older

409
Owning the bat model of your favorite player

410
Using your new bat for the first time

* * * * *

> The pitcher has got only a ball. I've got a bat.
> —Hank Aaron

* * * * *

411
Shoeless Joe Jackson named
his bat Black Betsy

412
Honus Wagner was
the first player to have his name
on a "Louisville Slugger"

413
When Richie Ashburn
was on a hot streak, he often
slept with his bat

414
Pete Browning, for whom
the first "Louisville Slugger"
was made, named each of his
hundreds of bats and "retired" them
after a prescribed number of hits

415
Babe Ruth would carve a notch
around the trademark of a bat
after he homered with it

* * * * *

416

Al Simmons swung the longest bat—
38 inches

417

Edd Rousch swung the heaviest bat—
48 ounces

418

Wee Willie Keeler swung
the shortest bat—30.5 inches

419

Solly Hemus swung the lightest bat—
29 ounces

420

Jim Rice once swung a bat so hard
that it broke in two, though he made
no contact with the ball

421

Some bats in the 19th century
came with guarantee cards stating that
if they broke, they could be returned

422
Going out with the gang to play ball

✳ ✳ ✳

✳ ✳ ✳

423
Getting a hit to impress the older kids

COMPLETING THE CIRCLE

When it was night he dragged the two halves of the bat into left field, and with his jacknife cut a long rectangular slash into the turf and dug out the earth. With his hands he deepened the grave in the dry earth and packed the sides tight. He then placed the broken bat in it. He couldn't stand seeing it in two pieces so he removed them and tried squeezing them together in the hope they would stick but the split was smooth, as if the bat had willed its own brokenness, and the two parts would not stay together. Roy undid his shoelaces and wound one around the slender handle of the bat, and the other he tied around the hitting part of the wood, so that except for the knotted laces and the split he knew was there it looked like a whole bat. And this was the way he buried it, wishing it would take root and become a tree. He poured back the earth, carefully pressing it down, and replaced the grass. He trod on it in his stocking feet, and after a last long look around, walked off the field.

—Bernard Malamud, *The Natural*

424
Rogers Hornsby

* * * * *

The best right-handed hitter
in baseball history

Has the highest lifetime average
in National League history—.358

Had the highest single-season average
in the 20th century—.424

Led the league in slugging percentage
a record 10 times

Is the only player other than
Ted Williams to win 2 Triple Crowns

Was disliked almost as much
as Ty Cobb

* * * * *

425
Reggie Jackson

* * * * *

Known as "Mr. October"
because he performed so well
in the postseason

Made history by hitting
3 home runs on 3 pitches
in a 1977 World Series
game vs the Dodgers

Was his own biggest fan
and loved being on center stage

Homered off the light tower at
Tiger Stadium in an All-Star Game

Was obnoxiously brash,
but got away with it
by being a winner

* * * * *

150

Baseball, it is
said, is only
a game. True.
And the Grand
Canyon is only
a hole in Arizona.
Not all holes,
or games, are
created equal.

—George F. Will

426 Pitchers working themselves into shape for the new season

★ ★ ★ ★ ★

427
A successful road trip

428
A long home stand

429
Veterans hanging on
for one more good year

430
The season yet to be played

★ ★ ★ ★ ★

431
A fastball smacking
into a mitt

432
A pitch that's so fast
that you hear but
don't see it

433
Throwing a pitch
that actually curves!

434
Your pitcher picks off
a runner who strays
too far off the base

435
A pitcher who stays in
the dugout to cheer on his
teammates after being removed
from the game, instead of
heading for the showers

436
The rare pitchers who
deliver the ball from the
side or underneath

437
The look of mingled relief
and delight when a pitcher
records the last out
of a no-hitter

438
Pitchers with
pinpoint control

439
Getting a batter out
by pitching him high and
inside to back him off the
plate and then low and
outside to have
him lunging

440
That you don't need strikes,
just the "illusion of strikes,"
to get batters to swing

441

Pitchers with a perfect
over-the-top delivery,
pitch after pitch

442

A pitcher and catcher
working their way through
the opposing lineup in
complete synchronicity

443

A "slurve"; something in
between a slider and a curve

444

The erratic movement
of a knuckleball, which makes
it hard to hit and catch

445

A split-fingered fastball
that drops straight down

446

Forkballs and palmballs
that throw off the
batter's timing

447

A left-handed pitcher
is called a "southpaw"

448

Seeing crafty pitchers
fooling batters

449

Lefties are usually the ones
who are called "wily" and
"crafty"

450
Pitchers and batters adjusting to each other
during the course of a game

451
Grover Cleveland Alexander returned to baseball
after fighting in WWI, despite suffering from shell shock,
partial hearing loss, and epilepsy

452
Hall of Fame pitcher Steve Carlton pretended
there was no batter and conducted a "sophisticated game
of catch" with his catcher

453
Pitcher Joey Jay was the first big leaguer
to have played in the Little League

454
Brothers Phil and Joe Niekro both were knuckleball pitchers

455
Joe Nuxhall was only 15 years old when he pitched
two-thirds of an inning for Cincinnati to become
modern baseball's youngest player

456
Workhorse pitchers

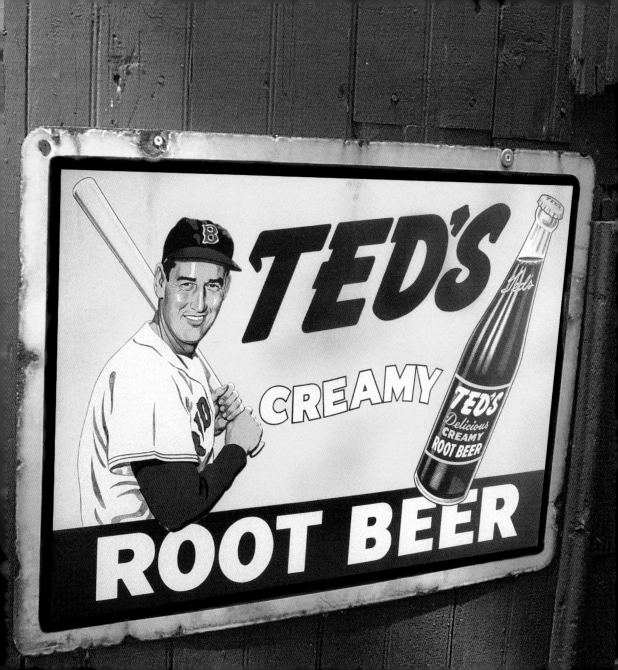

463
Sandy Koufax

* * * * *

Went to the University of Cincinnati
on a basketball scholarship

Joined the Dodgers in 1955
at the age of 15, but didn't become
a good pitcher until he stopped throwing
every pitch at 100 mph and learned to control
his fastball and his peerless curveball

Was baseball's dominant pitcher from 1962
to 1966, topping 300 strikeouts 3 times,
winning 5 consecutive ERA titles, and
leading the National League in wins,
ERA, and strikeouts 3 times

Threw 4 no-hitters and averaged
more than one strikeout an inning

Won 27 games in his last season
with a 1.73 ERA and retired
because of an arthritic pitching elbow

Had one weakness, according to
Whitey Ford—he couldn't hit

* * * * *

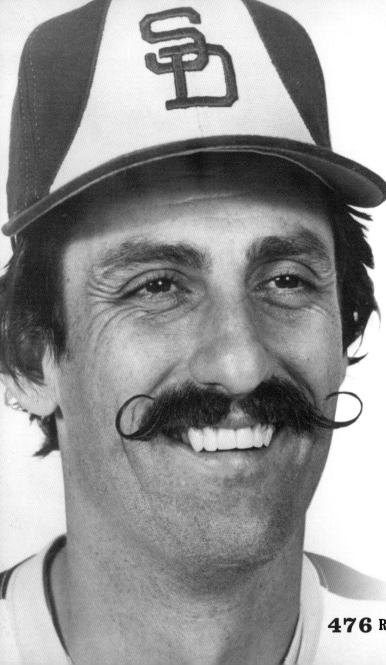

GREAT

★ ★ ★

NAMES

✶ ✶ ✶

477 Sixto Lezcano

478 Van Lingle Mungo

479 Enos Slaughter

480 Cesar Geronimo

481 Reno Bertoia

482 Catfish Metkovich

483 Minnie Minoso

484 Maurice Archdeacon

485 Damon Berryhill

486 Rivington Bisland

487 Rico Carty

488 Masanori Murakami

489 Vida Blue

490
Josh Gibson

* * * * *

Was the outstanding hitter
in the Negro Leagues

Smashed nearly 800 home runs,
including 75 in one season

May have hit a fair ball
out of Yankee Stadium,
which no major leaguer
ever did

* * * * *

GREAT BASEBALL WRITERS

★ ★ ★

491
Dave Anderson

492
Roger Angell

493
Thomas Boswell

494
Heywood Hale Broun

495
Jimmy Cannon

496
Frank Deford

497
Mike Downey

498
Peter Gammons

499
David Halberstam

500
Jerome Holtzman

501
Donald Honig

502
Roger Kahn

503
Mike Lupica

504
Terry Pluto

505
Shirley Povich

506
Grantland Rice

507
Lawrence S. Ritter

508
John Schulian

509
Dan Shaughnessy

510
Red Smith

511
George Vecsey

512
Roberto Clemente

Played with flair

Had a cannon for a throwing arm

Excelled in the World Series

Got his landmark 3,000th hit in his last at-bat

Died in a plane crash
while trying to deliver goods
to earthquake victims
in Nicaragua

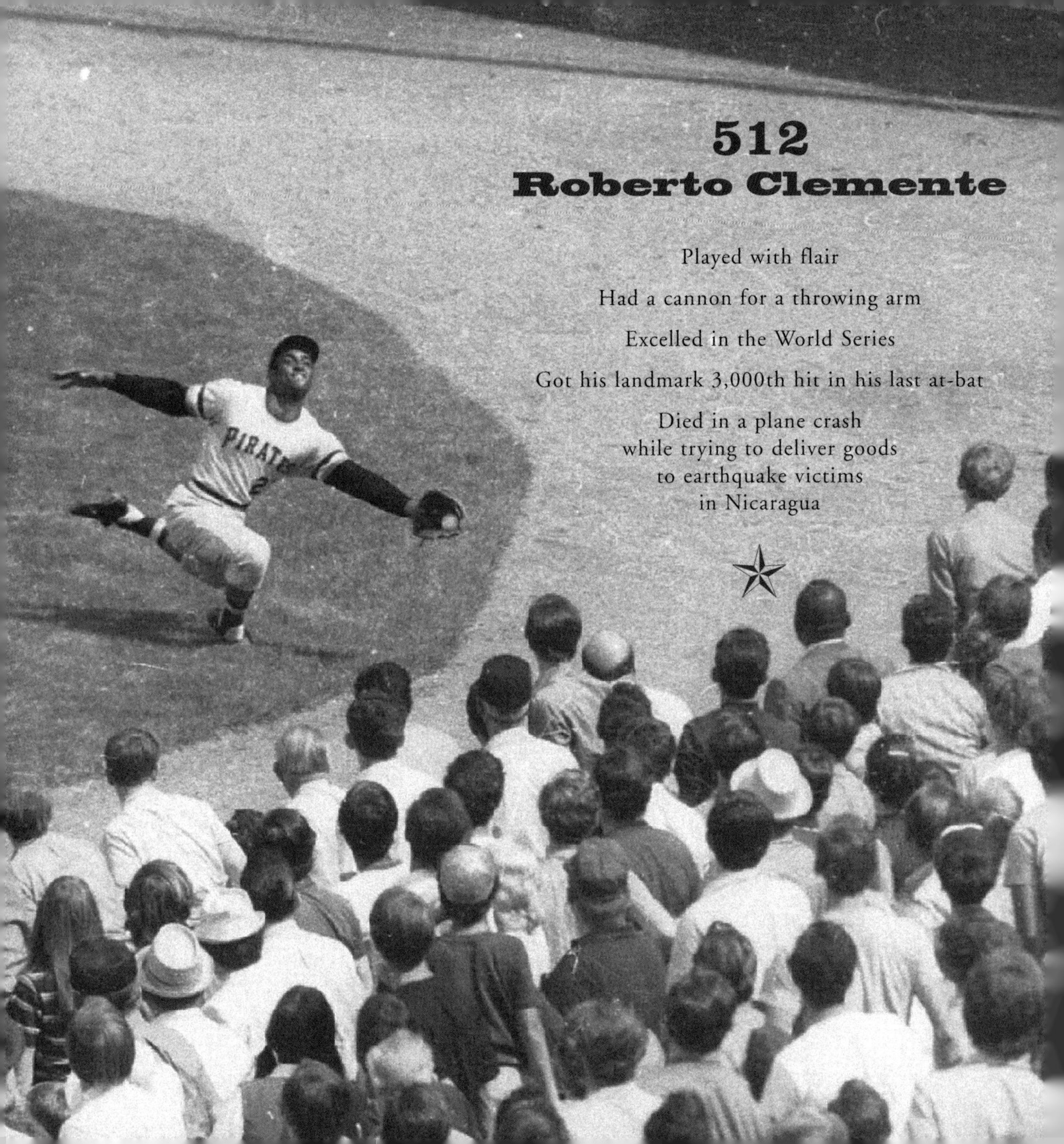

★

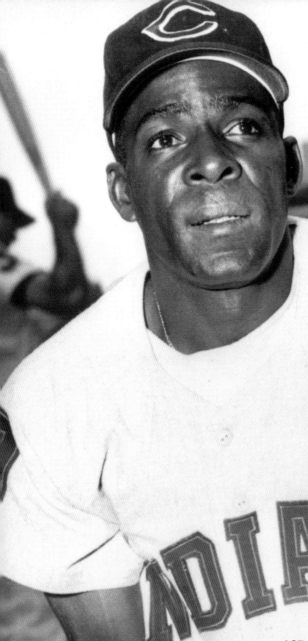

513
Minnie Minoso

Grew up in Cuba playing ball
and picking cotton

Was the first dark-skinned,
Latin American player to play
in the major leagues in 1949

Was the first black player to play
with the Chicago White Sox in 1951

Played with such flair that he became
the White Sox's most popular player
and owner Bill Veeck's favorite player

Led the American League in steals,
triples, and being hit by white pitchers

Had at least one at-bat in professional
baseball in each of 7 decades

✶　✶　✶　✶　✶

514

Babe Ruth

The most popular baseball player ever,
and according to most experts, the best

The American League's best left-handed pitcher,
who played for the Red Sox before becoming
a power-hitting outfielder with the Yankees

Was as flamboyant and charismatic
as he was talented

Walked through the streets of
New York trailed by young fans

Helped the Yankees win their first title
in 1923 and form a dynasty

Took baseball out of the dead-ball
era by slugging 60 homers in 1927
and 714 homers for his career,
both records

In 1927, out-homered the other
7 American League teams

His last home run cleared
the roof at Forbes Field
in Pittsburgh

✷   ✷   ✷

★ ★ ★ ★ ★

515
A daring steal of home

516
A timely pinch hit

517
When your pitcher
picks off a pinch runner

518
When your catcher
throws out a base stealer

519
Foiling a hit-and-run

★ ★ ★ ★ ★

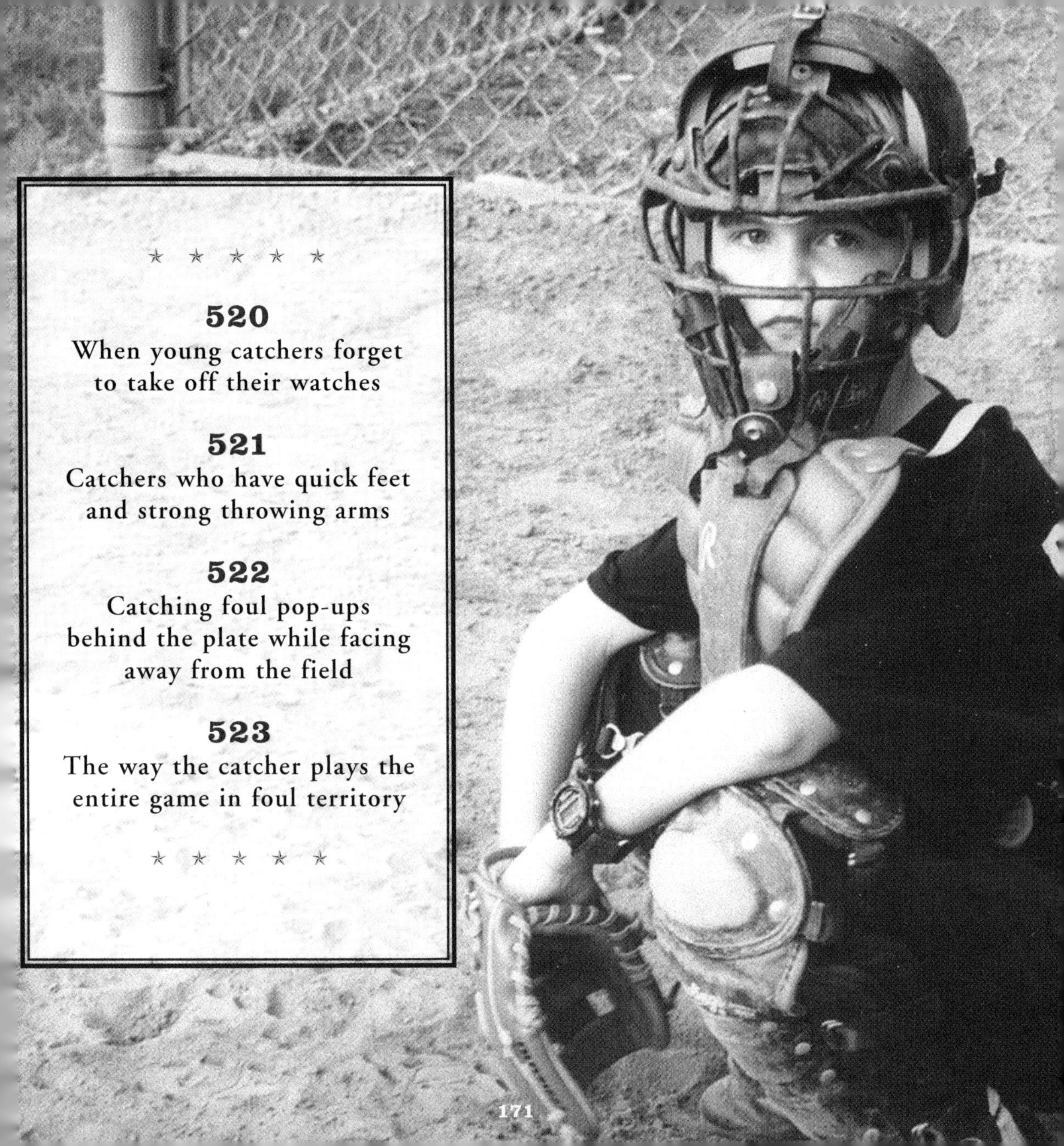

★ ★ ★ ★ ★

520
When young catchers forget
to take off their watches

521
Catchers who have quick feet
and strong throwing arms

522
Catching foul pop-ups
behind the plate while facing
away from the field

523
The way the catcher plays the
entire game in foul territory

★ ★ ★ ★ ★

Van Lingle Mungo

524

When a throw-in player in a trade becomes a star

525

A spectacular collision when no one is hurt

526

Clutch hitters and pitchers with ice water
in their veins

527

Explaining a balk to a foreigner

528

When a benchwarmer leads
the cheers in the dugout

529

Players who wear glasses

530

The infield fly rule

531

Stealing signs

★ ★ ★ ★ ★

532

A confident catcher controlling the game

★ ★ ★ ★ ★

★ ★ ★ ★ ★

541
When the catcher
blocks the plate

542
When the ump calls
it your way

543
When your entire family
sees you make the big play

544
The roar of the crowd

545
Seeing your name
in the newspaper

546
When you're the star
of the game

547 Watching your son pitch

548
High school baseball

549
Playing an outdoor game
in an urban setting

550
Representing your school or city

551
When the coach has given
you the ball

552
Imagining you are striking out
the greatest batters who ever lived

553
Playing in front of college recruiters

554
Beating your hated rivals

555
High socks

Oh, Doctor!

Hold the Phone!

Red Barber

BELOVED BASEBALL BROADCASTERS

✮ ★ ✮

556
Mel Allen

563
Bob Elson

571
Jon Miller

557
Red Barber

564
Curt Gowdy

572
Joe Morgan

558
Jack Brickhouse

565
Ernie Harwell

573
Lindsey Nelson

559
Frank Buck

566
Russ Hodges

574
Bob Prince

560
Joe Buck

567
Ralph Kiner

575
Rosey Rosewall

561
Harry Caray

568
Tony Kubek

576
Vin Scully

562
Bob Costas

569
Tim McCarver

577
Bob Uecker

570
Al Michaels

Harry Caray

578
The silver voice of Dodgers announcer Vin Scully

579
Lindsey Nelson, Bob Murphy, and Ralph Kiner broadcasting for the New York Mets for 17 years

580
Ernie Harwell's poetry

581
Announcers reading the disclaimer

582
Harry Caray's *"Holy Cow!"*

583
Mel Allen's home run call: *"That Ball is Going, Going, Gone!"*

584
Phil Rizzuto's *"Holy Cow!"*

585
Rosey Rosewall's home run call: *"Open the window, Aunt Minnie"*

586
Curt Gowdy and Tony Kubek on "Game of the Week"

587
Jon Miller and Joe Morgan on ESPN

588
Tim McCarver and Joe Buck on Fox

THE GIANTS WIN THE PENNANT!
THE GIANTS WIN THE PENNANT!
THE GIANTS WIN THE PENNANT!

THE GIANTS WIN THE PENNANT!
THE GIANTS WIN THE PENNANT!

—RUSS HODGES, 1951

George Sisler, Babe Ruth, and Ty Cobb

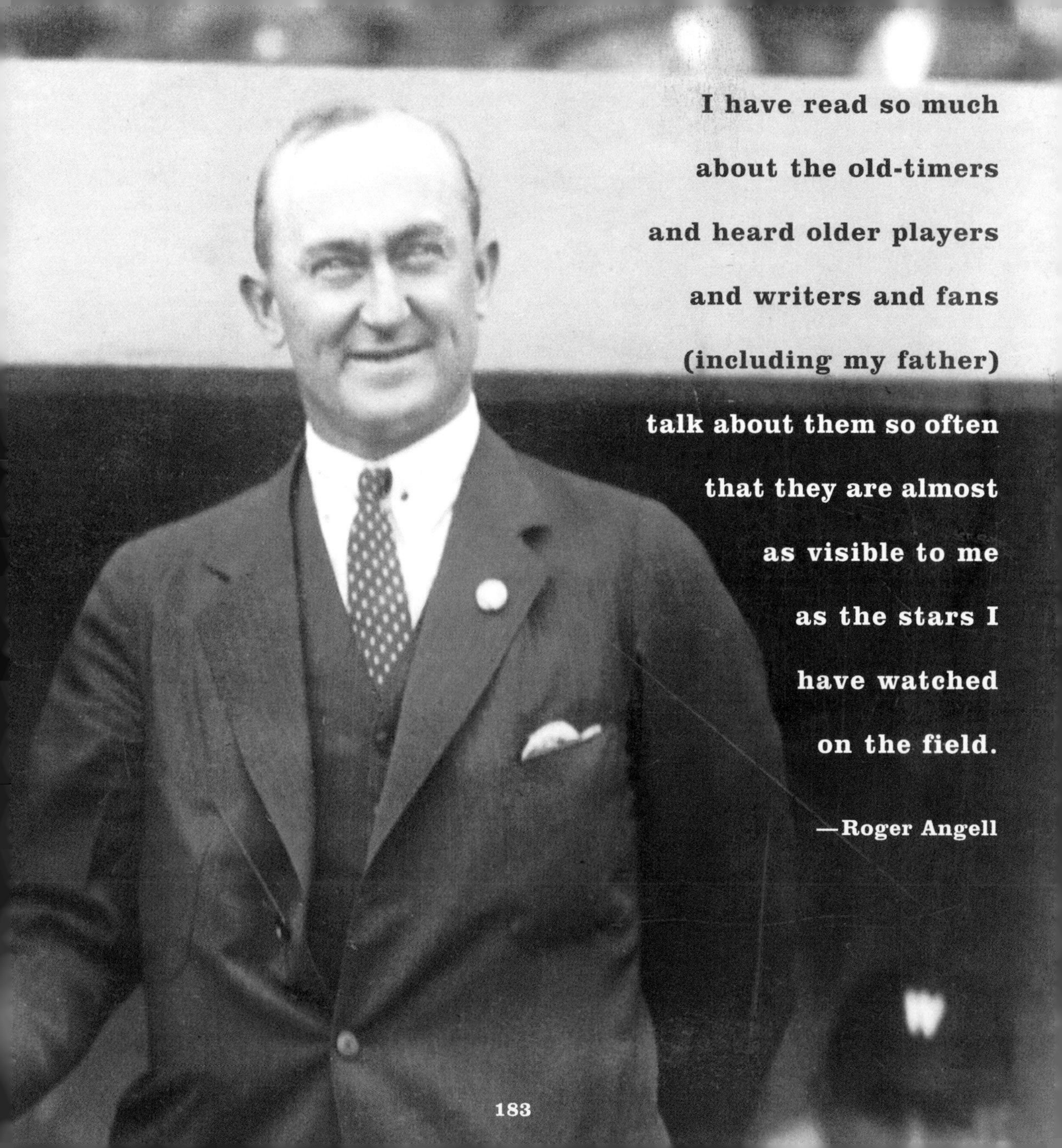

I have read so much
about the old-timers
and heard older players
and writers and fans
(including my father)
talk about them so often
that they are almost
as visible to me
as the stars I
have watched
on the field.

—Roger Angell

589
Joe DiMaggio

✮ ✮ ✮ ✮ ✮

Never made a mistake on the ballfield

Hit in 61 consecutive games
in the Pacific Coast League and a major league
record 56 games with the Yankees in 1941

Missed the first 65 games of the 1949 season
but returned to lead the Yankees to a 3-game sweep
of the rival Red Sox with 4 homers and 9 RBIs,
and propel his team to a world championship

Was baseball's best all-around player during his era

Was briefly married to Marilyn Monroe,
and after her death had a rose
placed at her grave every day

✮ ✮ ✮ ✮ ✮

THE BASEBALL TEN

* * * * *

In the long history of the game, a few brave souls stand out for taking on the establishment through words and actions. Here are ten who stood for positive change—or at least, freedom of expression.

590
Jim Bouton
Wrote controversial, behind-the-scenes books that showed baseball heroes as human, flaws and all

591
Curt Flood
Refused to be traded and jeopardized his career so that all players could have self-determination

592
Dave McNally and Andy Messersmith
Went to court to get rid of the reserve clause

593
Marvin Miller
Executive director of the Players Association, took on the owners and got equal power for his constituents

594
Jimmy Piersall
The one-time asylum inmate made management uneasy by always marching to his own exciting drumbeat

595
Vic Power
Was so flamboyant in the field and so outspoken that the Yankees traded him rather than have him as their first black player

596
Jackie Robinson
Withstood hostility and other tremendous pressures as the first African-American player in the majors

597
Bill Veeck
Was attacked by other owners for being consistently on the side of the fans

598
John Montgomery Ward
The Giants star was the president of baseball's first union, which championed exploited 19th-century players

* * * * *

Baseball is the belly of society. Straighten out baseball and you'll straighten out the rest of the world.

—Bill Lee

599
Reading box scores in the morning paper
and figuring out the entire game

600

The 2003 Red Sox broke
the 1927 Yankees' major league record
for slugging percentage

601

The 2003 Mariners made only
65 errors, a major league record

602

The Atlanta Braves have won
12 consecutive division titles

603

The New York Yankees have made
the postseason every year since 1995

604

The 1966 Dodgers and 2003 Mariners
are the only teams since 1904 to use
only 5 starting pitchers

BASEBALL GAME
WHITE EAGLES
vs.
SING SING PRISON NINE
At OSSINNING, N. Y.
Sunday, June 14th, 1936
Busses will leave Clubrooms, 595 E. Washington Av.
at 9:00 A. M. sharp   Rain or Shine.
ROUND TRIP TICKET $1.50
167

The Giants is dead.

—Chuck Dressen
 Dodgers manager, 1951

★ ★ ★ ★ ★

605
Willie McCovey's
tape-measure home runs

606
Carl Hubbell's screwball

607
Willie Mays's basket catch

608
The Giants' miraculous comeback
to win the 1951 pennant

★ ★ ★ ★ ★

He's the only guy who puts fear into me. Not because he can get me out, but because he could kill me.

—Reggie Jackson

609
Nolan Ryan

* * * * *

Struck out an incredible 5,714 batters
in his 27-year career—1,578 more than
runner-up Steve Carlton

Threw a record 7 no-hitters,
3 more than runner-up Sandy Koufax

Struck out a record 383 batters in 1973

At the age of 42, led the league in strikeouts
and at the age of 43, he became the oldest
pitcher to throw a no-hitter

Threw 100 mph in his prime
and 90 mph when he retired

Had his uniform retired by
the Angels, Astros, and Rangers

* * * * *

FIRST IMPRESSIONS

I'd never really sat down and watched a whole professional ball game on TV, but there was a big hayfield across the street where, every day the weather permitted, you played baseball. If you were a boy, that's what you did, like cows gave milk and Davy Crockett shot at bad guys. I was tall for my age and wouldn't go away, so I got to play with kids two, three, sometimes four years older, quantum leaps for a first-grader. This caused even more pressure to have opinions on teams and players. My brother liked the Yankees, so that was out, the Dodgers and Giants had already split for California, and the Mets hadn't made the scene yet. I chose the Pirates, I think because I liked their uniforms in the baseball-card pictures. Being a Pirates fan in upper New York State in the fifties wasn't as sociopathic as being a Cubs fan there (or being a Cubs fan anywhere), but it was unusual. So one day I turned on the TV and there was my favorite team, the Pittsburgh Pirates, in the uniforms I thought were so neat. I don't know whom they were playing or where, but it was late in the game when this big guy gets up and WHAM(!) wins it with a shot over the center-field wall. Way over. There was no instant replay in those days, but I feel like I saw it over and over again. And that was it—I was imprinted on Dick Stuart.

—John Sayles

610 Choosing sides

611
Roy
Campanella

* * * * *

Caught 4 games in a single
day for the Elite Giants
in the Negro Leagues

Was the first great black catcher
in the major leagues,
beginning in 1948

While catching for
the Brooklyn Dodgers,
won 3 National League
MVP awards

Was known for his sunny demeanor
while playing the game he loved

Drew a record 93,000 fans
to honor him on May 7, 1959
at the Los Angeles Coliseum,
a year after his playing career
ended when an auto accident
left him a quadriplegic

* * * * *

Was 18 when he joined
the Indians in 1936

Was the fastest pitcher
of his time

Also had the best
curveball of his time

Threw 3 no-hitters
and 11 one-hitters

612 Bob Feller

Pitched a no-hitter against the
White Sox on Opening Day in 1940

Won 266 games despite losing 4
seasons in his prime fighting in the war

Barnstormed after the season,
playing Negro League All-Star teams

★   ★   ★

613

Teammates greeting you
as you cross home plate

614

Home run races that go
down to the wire

615

Acquiring a superstar
in a big trade

616

Cleanup hitters

617

Good players who become
great managers

618

Hustling down the
first-base line

619

Winning with power
or speed

620

Curtain calls

Mark McGwire

BALLPLAYERS WITH ODD NAMES

★　★　★

621
SMEAD JOLLEY

622
HEINIE MANUSH

623
COONIE BLANK

624
WALLY SCHANG

625
OSSEE SCHRECKENGOST

626
ESTEL CRABTREE

627
JERRY SCHYPINSKI

628
NELLIE WOLFGANG

629
ED ZMICH

630
BOOB FOWLER

631
LYMAN LAMB

632
BRUNO BLOCK

633
BUNNY BRIEF

634
VIRGIL STALLCUP

635
BALDY LOUDEN

636
CLYDE KLUTTZ

637
COLONEL SNOVER

638
CANNONBALL TITCOMB

639
ALOYSIUS BEJMA

640
FATTY BRIODY

641
SIBBY SISTI

642
DEBS GARMS

643
COOT VEAL

* * * * *

644

Minor league park fences
advertising local businesses

645

Low ticket prices
at minor league games

646

Seeing promising young players
before they move up to
the big leagues

647

Feeling civic pride in your
local minor league team

* * * *

GREAT BASEBALL BOOKS

★　★　★

648
Ball Four
by Jim Bouton
and Leonard Shecter

649
Summer of '49
and *October 1964*
by David Halberstam

650
The Glory of Their Times
by Lawrence S. Ritter

651
The Long Season
and *Pennant Race*
by Jim Brosnan

652
*Tim McCarver's Baseball
for Brain Surgeons and
Other Fans*
by Tim McCarver

653
*Baseball's Great
Experiment*
by Jules Tygiel

654
The Boys of Summer
by Roger Kahn

655
Veeck as in Wreck
by Bill Veeck

656
Willie's Time
by Charles Einstein

657
Babe
by Robert Creamer

658
A False Spring
by Pat Jordan

659
The Summer Game
by Roger Angell

660
El Beisbol
by John Krich

661
The Wrong Stuff
by Bill Lee and Dick Lally

662
Eight Men Out
by Eliot Asinof

663
I Was Right on Time
by Buck O'Neil

664
Moneyball
by Michael Lewis

GREAT BASEBALL NOVELS

665
The Natural
by Bernard Malamud

666
The Southpaw
by Mark Harris

667
Bang the Drum Slowly
by Mark Harris

668
Shoeless Joe
by W.P. Kinsella

669
Screwballs
by Jay Cronley

670
The Universal Baseball Association, Inc. J. Henry Waugh, Prop.
by Robert Coover

671
The Bingo Long Traveling All-Stars and Motor Kings
by William Brashler

672
The Plot to Kill Jackie Robinson
by Donald Honig

673
You Know Me Al
by Ring Lardner

Baseball Trivia Answers

* * * * *

A Harry Frazee

B Billy Pierce (1.97 in 1955)

C Pittsburgh Pirates and Brooklyn Dodgers

D Tracy Stallard

E "The Big Cat"

F Roy Campanella

G They pitched baseball's only double no-hitter through 9 innings—Vaughn lost his no-hitter and the game in the 10th inning. Toney pitched a 10-inning complete game no-hitter.

H Tom House, a Braves reliever who was in the bullpen

I Harry Steinfeldt

J Tony Gwynn (.394 in 1994)

See page 77 for questions

BALLPLAYERS NAMED CHICK

* * * * *

It was a grand old name for the grand old game, from the earliest days of baseball up until the early 1940s. Then it seemed to wane, along with bowler hats, garters, and spitballs. They played their way into the record books but, mysteriously, there was not a catcher or third-baseman among them.

674 Chick Autry
Boston, first base

675 Chick Carroll
Washington, outfield

676 Chick Davies
Philadelphia, outfield

677 Chick Evans
Boston, pitcher

678 Chick Fewster
New York, second base

679 Chick Fraser
Philadelphia, pitcher

680 Chick Fullis
New York, outfield

681 Chick Fuhrmer
Cincinnati, shortstop

682 Chick Galloway
Philadelphia, shortstop

683 Chick Gandil
Washington, first base

684 Chick Hafey
St. Louis, outfield

685 Chick Keating
Chicago, shortstop

686 Chick King
Detroit, outfield

687 Chick Maynard
Boston, shortstop

688 Chick Pedroes
Chicago, outfield

689 Chick Robataille
Pittsburgh, pitcher

690 Chick Shorten
Detroit, outfield

691 Chick Smith
Cincinnati, pitcher

692 Chick Stahl
Boston, outfield

693 Chick Tolson
Chicago, first base

694 Stealing a base

695 Racing around the bases

696 Beating the throw to first

697 Scoring from second base on a single

698 Racing to third from first on a hit-and-run play

699 Scoring all the way from first base on a double

700 Hearing the girls in the stands chanting your name

701 Taking the extra base

702 Having all your family members present when you make your Little League debut

703 Winning a trophy

704 Pretending you are at bat and facing the game's best pitcher with two outs and a three-run deficit in the ninth inning of the seventh game of World Series—and you hit a home run with the bases loaded as the crowd goes wild!

Throw strikes.
Home plate
don't move.

—Leroy "Satchel" Paige

705
Leroy "Satchel" Paige

* * * * *

The greatest pitcher of the Negro Leagues

Pitched 55 no-hitters and as many as 2,500 games
before 10 million spectators in the Negro Leagues,
and while barnstorming in the United States
and Latin America

Threw with numerous windups, at different angles,
and with an endless assortment of pitches,
all with pinpoint control

As a 42-year-old rookie, helped the Cleveland Indians
win the world championship

The oldest All-Star in 1953

Pitched 3 scoreless innings for the Athletics at the age of 59

Spun yarns and gave advice on pitching and life

* * * * *

KNOTHOLE DREAMS

Bleacher seats at Ebbets Field cost fifty-five cents... If you had $1.10, you bought a general-admission ticket and sat almost anywhere ... Without money, you could still assault the ball park. In the deepest corner of right center-field, 399 feet from home plate, the concrete wall gave way to two massive iron doors, called collectively the Exit Gate. The base of the doors did not come flush against the ground. Lying prone on the slanting sidewalk of Bedford Avenue, you looked under a crack, twice as wide as an eyeball, and saw center field, left field and two-thirds of the infield. First base lay beyond the sight line, but if you cared enough, you learned to tell whether the man was safe at first by the reactions of the other players. If a man was out at first base, nobody ran to cover second. You had no choice but to learn the game. A sidewalk position was comfortable, except when wind lifted dirt from the outfield and swirled it under the gate and into your eyes, or a policeman poked a shoe into your ribs and said, "On your feet. Move." Then you muttered, "Weren't you ever a kid yourself?"

—Roger Kahn, *The Boys of Summer*

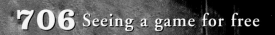

707 Pacific Bell Park (now SBC Park), San Francisco

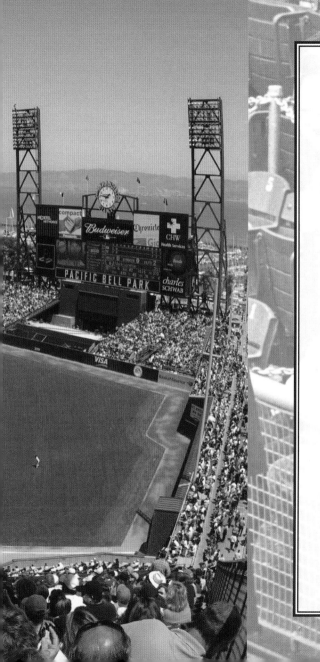

MUST-SEE STADIUMS

708
The Ballpark at Arlington, Texas

709
Coors Field, Denver

710
Fenway Park, Boston

711
Jacobs Field, Cleveland

712
Oriole Park at Camden Yards,
Baltimore

713
PNC Park, Pittsburgh

714
Wrigley Field, Chicago

715
Yankee Stadium, New York

GREAT BASEBALL SONGS

716
*Talkin' Baseball
(Willie, Mickey, and
the Duke)*
by Terry Cashman

717
*Say Hey
(The Willie Mays Song)*
by the Treniers

718
*A Dying Cub Fan's
Last Request*
by Steve Goodman

719
Cheap Seats
by Alabama

720
Van Lingle Mungo
by Dave Frishberg

721
The St. Louis Browns
by Skip Battin

722
I Love You, Mickey
by Teresa Brewer

723
The Greatest
by Kenny Rogers

724
Joltin' Joe DiMaggio
by Les Brown

725
The Ballad of Bill Lee
by Warren Zevon

726
Centerfield
by John Fogerty

727
Take Me Out to the Ball Game
Sung by fans in the stadium

MEMORABILIA

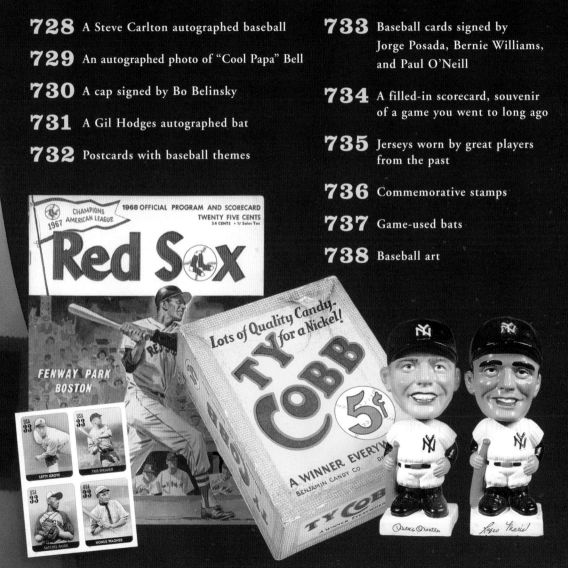

Willie Mays, Hank Aaron

739
Living legends

✶ ✶ ✶ ✶ ✶

You didn't let Willie Mays hit the first pitch.

Of course, he could hit the second pitch, too.

Willie liked to extend his arms like Duke

Snider, Mickey Mantle, and other power-

hitters, so if you crowded him with

one pitch and then threw him a pitch

low and away you could give him trouble.

Of course, you could pitch God that way,

it would give Him trouble.

—Don Newcombe

740 Spending hours touring the Hall of Fame in Cooperstown, New York

741 The annual Hall of Fame induction ceremony

742 You're stuck in traffic and a game comes on the radio

743 You have nothing to do, and the game is on TV

744 Naming your children or pets after ballplayers

745 Discovering that a major leaguer like Jim Fridley from Philippi, West Virginia, was born in your small hometown

Jim Fridley

746
Cal Ripken, Jr.

★ ★ ★ ★ ✩

Played in an amazing 2,632 consecutive games

Had an inspirational work ethic

Always made himself available to sign autographs

Made only 3 errors one season at shortstop

Paved the way for Alex Rodriguez, Derek Jeter,
Nomar Garciaparra, and other tall, power-hitting shortstops

Was twice voted the American League's MVP, 8 seasons apart

Hit a dramatic home run in his final All-Star Game before
his retirement, to earn selection as the MVP of the game

★ ★ ★ ★ ✩

747 A hook slide that eludes the tag

Ty Cobb

748
Sliding hard into second base
to break up a double play

749
Sliding under the tag

750
A proper, feet-first, pop-up slide
into a base

751
A hustling batter beating it down
the line to get an infield hit

752
A third-base coach windmilling
his arm to signal a runner speeding
toward third to go on home

753
Runners taking off with
the crack of the bat

754
An exciting double steal

★ ★ ★ ★ ★

755

A tape-measure home run

★ ★ ★

756

An opposite-field homer

757

A booming grand slam

758

Smashing a ball over
an outfielder's head

759

When a once-great hitter
returns to form

760

A slumping batter wisely hitting
the ball up the middle

761

Unloading on a curve or slider

762

A ball exploding off the bat
and going into orbit

763

Slugfests

The greatest thrill in the world is to end the game with a home run and watch everybody walk off the field while you're running the bases on air.

—Al Rosen

764 A great base stealer

765

"5-tool players"—players who can hit for average, hit with power, run, catch, and throw

766

A player who has failed redeeming himself the next day; maybe even his next time at bat

767

A runner who is alert enough to take the next base on a short passed ball or wild pitch

768

When a small-budget team has a better season than a major-market team

769

Moving into first place

770

Scrappy overachievers

771

When the hero of the game is the seldom-used backup player who is filling in for an injured star

772

The rare players who throw left-handed and bat right-handed

773
Pete Rose

* * * * *

Nicknamed "Charlie Hustle"

Ran to first when he was walked

Made the All-Star team
at 5 positions

Dove into third base

Got hits in a National League-record
44 consecutive games

Cried on the field
after breaking Ty Cobb's
all-time record for base hits

Has always been beloved
by baseball fans

* * * * *

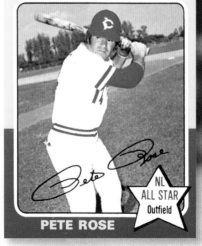

PETE ROSE

SURPRISING HEROES

774

Dusty Rhodes, 1954

The unexpected star of the World Series
led the New York Giants to a 4-game
sweep of the Cleveland Indians

775
Bobo Holloman, 1953
Holloman, 29-year old St. Louis Browns rookie reliever, was about to be sent to the minors, but instead became the 3rd major leaguer to throw a no-hitter in his first start.

776
Don Larsen, 1956
Larsen, journeyman pitcher of the Yankees, threw a perfect game against the Brooklyn Dodgers in the World Series.

777
Bob "Hurricane" Hazle, 1957
Hazle, who, while replacing an injured starter, batted an astronomical .403 with 7 homers in 134 at-bats to help the Milwaukee Braves win the pennant.

778
Cookie Lavagetto, 1947
Lavagetto, the Dodgers pinchhitter, got his last major league hit—a 2-RBI double that broke up Bill Bevens's no-hit bid with 2 outs in the 9th inning to give the Dodgers a 3-2 victory in Game 4 of the World Series.

779
Bucky Dent, 1978
Dent, the Yankees' light-hitting shortstop, hit an unexpected 3-run homer off Red Sox Mike Torrez to erase a 2-0 deficit in the 7th inning and propel the Yankees to a pennant-winning victory in a one-game playoff.

780
Francisco Cabrera, 1992
Cabrera's 2-out pinch hit single in the 9th inning drove in the tying and winning runs in Game 7 of the NLCS to give the Atlanta Braves the National League pennant over the Pittsburgh Pirates.

781
Scott Brosius, 1998
Brosius, the A's third baseman, after hitting .203 in 1997, was shipped to the Yankees, and in 1998 was the MVP of the World Series.

782
Aaron Boone, 2003
Struggling Boone hit an 11th-inning walk-off home run against the Red Sox in Game 7 of the ALCS to give the Yankees the pennant.

QUIRKS, TRAITS,

783 The unorthodox, twisting windups of Luis Tiant, Fernando Valenzuela, and Hideo Nomo

784 Ozzie Smith doing a backflip during his pre-game routine

785 Ron Cey running like a penguin

786 Mel Ott's high-leg kick

787 Ewell Blackwell's sidearm delivery

788 Alfonso Soriano chomping on his gum

789 Joe Morgan flapping his back elbow up and down like a chicken while waiting for a pitch

790 The range and arm of Hall of Fame shortstop Luis Aparicio

791 Andy Pettitte's lethal pickoff move

Luis Tiant

AND INTANGIBLES

Juan Marichal

Derek Jeter's winning attitude

Jackie ROBINSON

second base BROOKLYN DODGERS

The way I figured it, I was even
with baseball and baseball with me.
The game had done much for me,
and I had done much for it.

—Jackie Robinson

807 Jackie Robinson

Broke baseball's
color barrier in 1947
with the Brooklyn Dodgers

Withstood tremendous hostility
from fans and opponents and
became the National League's
first Rookie of the Year

Starred in track, football,
and basketball in high school
and college

Was the driving force behind
the Dodgers' pennants in 1947,
1949, 1952, 1953, 1955,
and 1956

Retired, rather than accept
being traded to the Giants,
the Dodgers' hated rivals

Became a heroic symbol for
progress in baseball and America

ENCOURAGING WORDS

* * * * *

808
"Good eye!"

809
"It only takes one!"

810
"A walk is as good as a hit!"

811
"Keep your eye on the ball!"

812
"Swing batter, batter, batter"

813
"Make him throw a strike!"

814
"Hang in there!"

* * * * *

815 Willie Mays

Was the most exciting ballplayer of all time, according to many fans

Was also the best all-around ballplayer of his era

Hit 660 career homers, and twice hit more than 50 in a season, despite playing in the huge Polo Grounds and windy Candlestick Park

Flew around the bases as his hat fell off

Made basket catches and chased down balls hit over his head in center field

Played stick ball with the kids of Harlem

Greeted everyone with a happy "Say Hey"

Yogi Berra

FIELDING

* * * * *

816

A throw from the outfield that guns
down the runner at home plate

817

Those rare left-handed catchers

818

Catchers running down the line
on grounders to back up first base
in case the throw goes awry

819

An exciting over-the-shoulder catch
while running away from home plate

820

The symmetry of the
"rotation play": To defense a bunt
with a man on second, the third
baseman and first baseman charge
the plate, the shortstop covers third,
the second baseman covers first

* * * * *

Jimmy Piersall

821

An outfielder jumping high
to catch a ball that was
heading over the fence

822

Snatching a line drive
out of the air

823

Outfielders running down
fly balls at top speed

824

When the opposing team's
defensive specialist makes
his only error of the season
to let the winning run score

* * * * *

825
A smoothly turned 6-4-3
double play, from the shortstop
to the second baseman
to the first baseman

826
A challenging 3-6-3
double play, from the first
baseman to the shortstop
and back to first

827
A fast-moving, around-the-
horn (third to second to first)
double play

828
A second baseman making
a nifty pivot on second base,
then throwing to first to
complete the double play

829
Infielders who save errors by
scooping up throws in the dirt

Nomar Garciaparra

830

The shortstop going into
the hole to make a brilliant
stab of a hard grounder and
making the long throw to nip
the batter at first

831

Utility players who learn to play
many positions to increase
their playing time

832

A nimble first baseman capturing
an errant throw from an
infielder to record the out

833

Charging in to field a grounder;
doing a crow hop on the throw
to first base

834

Catching a sizzling line drive
down the third-base line
at the Hot Corner

★ ★ ★ ★ ★

835 **A leaping catch**

Ken Griffey, Jr.

✳ ✳ ✳ ✳ ✳

836
A diving catch

837
A sliding catch

838
A great relay throw

839
When the potential
game-winning home run
ball hit by an opposing
player is deflected by the
wind and caught on
the warning track

840
Third basemen
making a difficult
barehanded pickup
on a slow grounder
to throw out the
batter at first

✳ ✳ ✳ ✳ ✳

841

Willie Mays, 1954

In the World Series, Willie Mays made an over-the-shoulder catch
of Vic Wertz's fly ball in dead center field at the Polo Grounds,
whirled around and made a perfect throw back to the infield
to prevent the base runners from advancing—the most
famous fielding play in baseball history.

FIELDING FEATS

* * * * *

842
Derek Jeter, 2001

In a remarkable heads-up play in the playoff series vs Oakland, he ran from his shortstop position all the way to the first base line to catch a wild throw and then backflip the ball to the catcher just in time to tag out the potential tying run.

843
Joe Rudi, 1972

Oakland's unsung left fielder made a sensational, game-saving catch with his outstretched glove against the fence in Game 2 of the World Series against the Reds.

844
Al Gionfriddo, 1947

Dodger outfielder Gionfriddo robbed Joe DiMaggio of a hit with a crucial one-handed catch while moving backward, 415 feet from home plate during the World Series—prompting the Yankee Clipper to kick up dirt, the only frustration he ever exhibited on the field.

845
Bill Wambsganss, 1920

The Cleveland second baseman recorded the only unassisted triple play in World Series history against Brooklyn, catching a line drive, stepping on second to double up a runner who had left the base, and then tagging out a second runner who had taken off from first.

846
Roger Maris, 1962

Maris made a sparkling defensive stop in right field in the 9th inning of the 7th game of the World Series that prevented the tying run from scoring.

847
Roger
Clemens

Worked harder than anybody
to stay in shape

Won five Cy Young awards

Was nicknamed "The Rocket"
because he threw so hard

Gave his kids names beginning
with "K," since K is how you
score a strikeout

Revived his career after everyone
said his arm was gone

Was the first pitcher to strike
out 20 batters in a 9-inning
game, and, amazingly, did it
again 10 years later

NOBODY'S ON YOUR SIDE FOR LONG

Refs, umps, anybody calling a game can't win. Put on that uniform and your IQ drops to zero and your vision goes along with it. Nobody's on your side for long. When I was a kid, my dad umpired softball games as well as some high school and American Legion baseball. He knew how it felt to be the clueless guy behind the plate. And yet when he took me to see the local pro team, he would sit in the stands and yell at the umpires like he had just hit his thumb with a hammer. It was only much later that I understood why Dad yelled at the umps. It's the same understanding that probably lets most arbiters go home and sleep peacefully after a good cussing out. They know that for the fans, it's an outlet, a chance to yell at the world.

—Ron Green

Mike Cameron

Ozzie Smith

DAZZLING SHORTSTOPS

* * * * *

849
Luis Aparicio and Willie Miranda

850
Roy McMillan and Jose Pagan

851
Bobby Wine and Ruben Amaro

852
Allan Trammell and Mark Belanger

853
Gene Alley and Dave Concepcion

854
Larry Bowa and Tony Fernandez

855
Ozzie Smith and Ozzie Guillen

856
Mike Bordick and Omar Vizquel

* * * * *

INSPIRING FIELDERS

★ ✯ ★

857
Vic Power and Keith Hernandez

First Basemen

858
Bill Mazeroski and Julian Javier

Second Basemen

859
Billy Cox and Brooks Robinson

Third Basemen

860
Al Kaline and Carl Furillo

Right Fielders

861
Gene Woodling and Carl Yastrzemski

Left Fielders

862
Tris Speaker and Curt Flood

Center Fielders

863
Jim Hegan and Johnny Bench

Catchers

864
Bobby Shantz and Jim Kaat

Pitchers

★ ★ ★ ★ ★

865
Slick infielders

866
Shagging flies

867
Closing your eyes
when the ball is coming
toward you—then, finding
the ball in your glove

868
Making a super defensive
play to impress the older kids

869
A good, strong,
accurate throw

870
Gobbling up grounders

871
An exciting
rundown play

★ ★ ★ ★ ★

The biggest change
in baseball since
the mid-fifties is
the improvement
of gloves.

—Ralph Kiner

GLOVES

* * *

872
The sharp, leathery smell of a new glove

873
Owning the model glove of your favorite player

874
The pancake-style gloves fielders wore
through the 1920s

875
"Bill Doak" model gloves, the first gloves
that had a real pocket

876
Hopeful kids bringing their gloves to the park
in case a ball comes their way

* ★ *

877
Putting on your brand new
glove for the first time

878
Breaking in a new glove
by repeatedly pounding it
with a ball

879
Playing catch with your dad

880 Getting your first glove for your birthday

Baseball is ninety percent mental
and the other half is physical.

—Yogi Berra

881
Yogi Berra

* * * * *

Was loved by all fans, even those
who hated the Yankees

Played on a team of stars,
yet was voted the American
League's MVP 3 times

Was the inspiration for the popular
cartoon character Yogi Bear

Read comic books while his
roommate Bobby Brown, a future
doctor, studied Gray's *Anatomy*

Was notorious for hitting
home runs on pitches that were
an inch off the ground
or a foot over his head

Refused to speak
to George Steinbrenner
for years after the Yankee owner
told him his job as manager
was secure and promptly had
someone else fire him

* * * * *

MY TIGER

I grew up in a home where the radio was permanently set on WJR; I thought George-Kell-and-Ernie-Harwell was one word. I'd fall asleep listening to my parents discussing the merits and flaws of various Detroit players, and by the time I was twelve I wanted one of my own, a Tiger, my very own player to root for and adore. In 1962, my goals in life were to be the first governor of Michigan and to marry Rocky Colavito. I was crazy about him, in love the way only a twelve-year-old who knows nothing about it can be. It was my love for him, rather than baseball, that led me to my first game at Tiger Stadium—that 22-inning, 7-hour marathon with the Yankees, which the Tigers lost despite Rocky's heroic 7 hits in 10 at-bats: more than Maris, Mantle, and Berra combined.

Seven hours was a long time for a preteen whose only interest in baseball was Rocky Colavito, but was I weary? Never. During the "boring parts" (i.e., when the Yankees were at bat), I sat happily carving ROCKY in the chest of a stuffed Tiger my father bought me to keep me quiet.

BASEBALL THRILLS

COLAVITO'S GREAT CATCH SAVES GAME

—Rebecca Stowe

882

Connie Mack, who managed and owned the Philadelphia Athletics from 1901 to 1950, always wore a suit and tie in the dugout

Connie Mack

MANAGERS

* * * * *

883

In the 1980s, A's manager Tony La Russa turned starter Dennis
Eckersley into a reliever and reliever Dave Stewart into a starter: they
both revived their careers and became big stars for their new team

884

Joe Torre made it to the World Series as a manager with the Yankees
in 1996, after a record of 4,272 games as a player and manager
without participating in the Fall Classic

885

The pre-game exchange of lineups at home plate,
usually by the opposing managers

* * * * *

* * * * *

886
Frank Robinson, baseball's first
black manager

887
In the early 60s, the lowly Cubs tried
having the team run by several coaches rather
than a manager—and failed to improve

888
Managers who feign tranquility
while sitting in the dugout, although
their stomachs are madly churning

889
The legend of John McGraw

890
Making out a lineup

* * * * *

When all is said and done,
all I want anyone to say of me is,
Earl Weaver—he sure was
a good sore loser.

—Earl Weaver

Earl Weaver

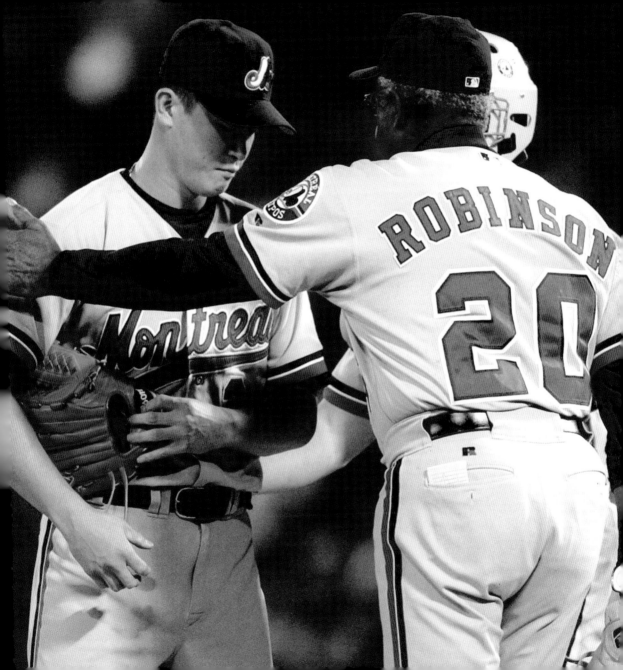

891
Casey Stengel

✶ ✶ ✶ ✶ ✶

Was one of the real characters of the game

Managed the Yankees from 1949 to 1960,
winning 10 pennants and 7 World Series

Put out to pasture because of his age,
he became the first manager of the cellar-dwelling
but beloved New York Mets

Spoke in doubletalk, rarely used punctuation,
forgot players' names, and spoke in a strange language
dubbed "Stengelese"

Talked endlessly to reporters to keep
the pressure off his players

Had his number retired by both
the Yankees and Mets

✶ ✶ ✶ ✶ ✶

**The secret of managing is to keep
the guys who hate you away from
the guys who are undecided.**

—Casey Stengel

892
An umpire shouting, "Play ball!"

893
An umpire brushing off home plate
with his tiny broom

894
A deep-voiced umpire whose calls
of "Ball" and "Strike!" reverberate
throughout the stadium

895
Umpires trying to break up
a lengthy meeting on the mound

896
An entertaining, nose-to-nose
argument between a manager
and an umpire

897
In 1956, Ed Rommell became
the first umpire to dare wear glasses
on the field

They expect the umpire to be perfect on Opening Day and to improve as the season goes on.

—Umpire Nestor Chylak

898
Daytime baseball
at Wrigley Field

* * * * *

899
The ivy that covers the outfield fence

900
Wrigley's loyal, boisterous bleacher bums

901
The bleacher bums throwing
the visitors' home run balls
back onto the field

902
Watching the game from
the neighboring rooftops

903
The home runs that fly
onto Waveland Avenue

* * * * *

OLD BALLPARKS

* * * * *

904
Briggs Field, Detroit

905
League Park, Cleveland

906
The Polo Grounds, New York

907
Sportsman's Park, St. Louis

908
Comiskey Park, Chicago

909
Ebbets Field, Brooklyn

910
Forbes Field, Pittsburgh

* * * * *

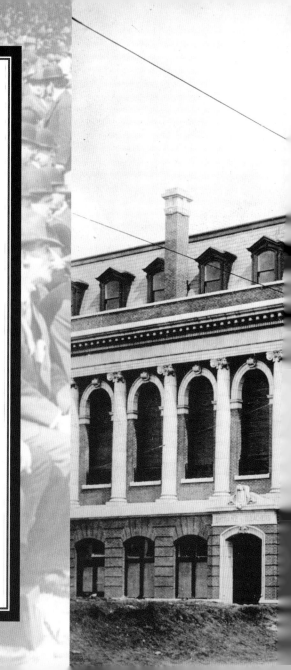

911 Shibe Park, Philadelphia

THE WHOLE PARK
WAS UP YELLING

I was groggy but saw an opening. I dashed in and then up and down the third-base line with three infielders and the catcher after me. I was in a hotbox... finally, Jim Delahanty caught up, slammed the ball into the small of my back. The force of that on top of my [earlier] exertions and the terrific heat all but knocked me out... I sprawled forward. After tagging me Delahanty dropped the ball. It rolled loose. I was out, but could see the plate three feet away. They said I looked like a wounded crab as I crawled toward it, using my fingernails ... the whole park was up yelling.

—Ty Cobb

MORE OLD BALLPARKS

912
Astrodome, Houston

913
Baker Bowl, Philadelphia

914
Braves Field, Boston

915
Candlestick Park,
San Francisco

916
Crosley Field, Cincinnati

917
Gilmore Field, Hollywood

918
Wrigley Field, Los Angeles

919
Hilltop Park, New York

920
Memorial Stadium,
Cleveland

921
Metropolitan Stadium,
Minneapolis

922
Municipal Stadium,
Kansas City

923
Offerman Stadium, Buffalo

924
Griffith Stadium,
Washington

925

When your best friend
roots for the other team

926

When friends say they
saw you on TV

927

Beating your brother
to the sports page
to read the scores

928

When it turns out your
crush is a baseball fan

929

Spending hours playing
APBA or Strato-matic
table-top baseball games

930

Reading batting averages
of every major leaguer
in the Sunday paper

938

Mickey Mantle

Did the impossible and replaced Joe DiMaggio in center field for the New York Yankees

Became the hero of thousands of baseball fans in the 1950s and 1960s, and still is the most popular figure on post-WWII baseball cards

Smashed numerous tape-measure homers, including one that went a record 565' in Washington, and came closer than anyone to hitting a ball out of Yankee Stadium

Won the Triple Crown in 1956, and 3 MVP awards, and hit over 50 homers in a season twice

Played almost his entire career despite painful leg injuries

Along with Willie Mays, was a symbol of an era

Baseball was my whole life.
Nothing's ever been as fun
as baseball.

—Mickey Mantle

939 **Tickets to the World Series**

940

A present of box seats
to the big game

941

The excitement of entering
a major league park through
the turnstiles

942

Retired uniform numbers
adorning the fences of
major league parks

943

Striking up a baseball chat
or a friendly argument with
a fan in the next row

944

Fans cheering former heroes
who were traded away but return
on the opposing team

945

Batters in their home parks
who wave to cheering fans
after a big home run

946

Filling in All-Star ballots
at the ballpark

947

Baseball fans like
the Ticket Lady

✷ ✷✷ ✷

948
Watching batting practice

949
Getting to the stadium early,
when the stands are empty

✷ ✷✷ ✷

A hot dog at the ballpark is better than steak at the Ritz.

—Humphrey Bogart

★ ★ ★ ★ ★

950
A really, *really* great hot dog
and a cold drink

951
The vendor of your favorite snack
finally comes by

952
Eating a full bag of shelled peanuts

★ ★ ★ ★ ★

* * * * *

953
Everything smells and tastes
better at the ballpark

954
Cotton candy, crackerjacks,
and other snacks have nutritional value
when eaten at the ballpark

955
Vendors shouting, "Peanuts!"
and "Beeer Heeer!"

956
Sushi!

* * * * *

957
Leaving work early
to go to the ballpark

958 Dressing in style for the game

959
Snagging the
perfect seat

960
Being there
with the guys

961
When the cheering
drowns out the boos

962
Taking Dad to the
game on Father's Day

963
Fancy patterns on freshly mowed outfield grass

964
Excitedly looking over the new baseball schedule
to see which games you want to attend

965
When the crowd goes wild after a home run

966
Having the only kids in the entire ballpark
who aren't sick from overeating

967
Having the only dad in the ballpark
who isn't a loudmouth

968
A full-house crowd rising to its feet

969
Pennants flying around the stadium

970
Bobble-head Give-away Day

971
Your team's mascot

972 Watching the big game with other fans at a sports bar

973
Listening to the game on the radio
while you are at the beach

974
Meeting someone with similar
baseball memories

975
Listening to a game late at night,
in bed, under the covers

976
Checking the morning papers
for the standings and the leagues'
statistical leaders

977
Finding *Baseball Weekly*
in your mailbox

978
A beach full of radios,
all tuned to the same game

★ ★ ★ ★ ★

979

Remembering the kids you
once played ball with

980

Sitting on the bench
with your teammates

981

Awaiting your turn at bat

982

Pitchers trying the
"drop" pitch

983

Fielders trying the
"hidden-ball" trick

984

Win or lose, your team
goes out for pizza or
burgers after the game

* * *

985

Emerging from a dark passageway
into the brightly-lit stadium

986

The pitcher tipping his cap
to the cheering fans as he heads
for the dugout

987

Getting an autograph
at the ballpark

988

Abbott and Costello's classic
comedy routine, "Who's on First?"

989

All-Star Games introductions

990

Fans' marriage proposals shown
on the electric scoreboard

991

Fans who won't do the Wave

992

The foul-mouthed heckler
behind you being escorted
from the ballpark

993

Getting your favorite
team's yearbook

994

Players getting married
at home plate

995

Ladies' Day

THE POLO GROUNDS
WENT UNDER LAST WEEK

The things I liked best about the Polo Grounds were sighs and emotions so inconsequential that they will surely slide out of my recollection. A flight of pigeons flashing out of the barn-shadow of the upper stands, wheeling past the right-field foul pole, and disappearing above the inert, heat-heavy flags on the roof. The steepness of the ramp descending from the Speedway toward the upper-stand gates, which pushed your toes into your shoe tips as you approached the park, tasting sweet anticipation and getting out your change to buy a program. The unmistakably

final "Plock!" of a line drive hitting the green wooden barrier above the stands in deep left field. The gentle, rocker like swing of the loop of rusty chain you rested your arm upon in a box seat, and the heat of the sun-warmed iron coming through your shirtsleeve under your elbow. At a night game, the moon rising out of the scoreboard like a spongy, day-old orange balloon and then whitening over the waves of noise and the slow, shifting clouds of floodlit cigarette smoke. All these I mourn, ...

—Roger Angell, *The Summer Game*

996 Lou Gehrig

Today I consider myself the luckiest man on the face of the earth.

—Lou Gehrig

★ ★ ★

Was one of the most beloved players in baseball history

Batted behind Babe Ruth in the Yankees' "Murderers Row"

Called the "Iron Horse" for playing 2,130 consecutive games as the first baseman for the New York Yankees

Attended Columbia University, loved ballet and opera, and spoke out against prejudice

Was the first player to have his uniform number retired

Hit a record 23 grand slams and drove in an American League-record 184 runs in a season

Died of amyotrophic lateral sclerosis, which has since been called "Lou Gehrig's Disease"

★ ★ ★

997
The long season,
from March to October

999
A thrilling, 7-game
World Series

998
The playoffs

1000
A victory parade

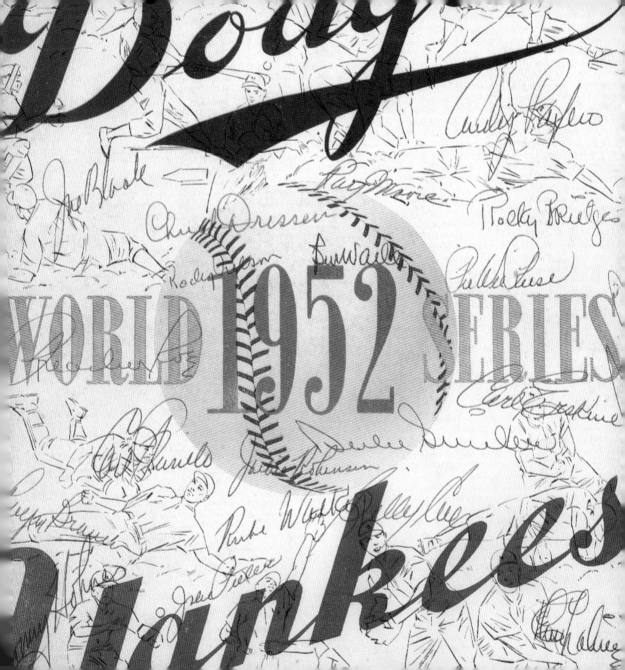

People ask
me what I
do in winter
when there's
no baseball.
I'll tell you
what I do.
I stare out
the window
and wait
for spring.

—Rogers Hornsby

Cool Papa Bell

★ ★ ★

ACKNOWLEDGMENTS

Thanks to everyone who helped us bring this labor of love to fruition. Most of all we thank Anne Kostick (a Cyclones booster), our truly inspiring editor and captain; Dave Green (a Red Sox supporter), who designed this book with incredible skill and creativity; our publisher Leslie Stoker (a devoted Yankees fan), who shares our passion for this great American game; and our relentless photo editor Anne Kerman (an admirer of Roger Maris), who tracked down everyone from Van Lingle Mungo to Rollie Fingers to kids eating hot dogs. Thanks go to the staff of Stewart, Tabori & Chang for all their help, particularly Jack Lamplough, Trudi Bartow, and Carmen Botez.

Special thanks to: Tom Butkier, Hudson Valley Renegades; W.C. Burdick, National Baseball Hall of Fame Library; Joanne Cornelius, Cleveland State University Library; Scott Jordan-Levy; Peter Avalos, Lelands.com; B.Quick Chadwick, Russell Athletic (WestWayne, Inc.); Clay Luraschi, Topps Company, Inc.; Kevin O'Sullivan, Associated Press; and AAGPBL-Players Association.

We are most grateful for the support and encouragement of Hubert Pedroli (a recent baseball convert); Ron Green Sr.; Mary Mathwich; A's fan Jeanie Dooha; Twins fan Elinor Nauen; Tigers fan Rebecca Stowe; diehard Mets fan Suzanne Rafer; broadcaster Tim McCarver; and everyone at RLR, Ltd., especially Jennifer Unter, Tara Mark, Gail Lockhart, Maury Gostfrand, Barbara Hadzicosmas, and Robert L. Rosen.